CUTTING THE WIRE

CUTTING THE WIRE

Photographs and Poetry from the US-Mexico Border

Photographs by Bruce Berman
Poetry by Ray Gonzalez and Lawrence Welsh
Edited by Lisa McNiel
Introduction by David Dorado Romo

University of New Mexico Press • Albuquerque

Printed in Malaysia

Library of Congress Cataloging-in-Publication Data
Names: Berman, Bruce, photographer. | McNiel, Lisa, editor. | Romo, David Dorado, writer of introduction. | Gonzalez, Ray, poems. Selections. | Welsh, Lawrence, 1959– Poems. Selections.
Title: Cutting the wire: photographs and poetry from the US-Mexico border / photographs by Bruce Berman; poetry by Ray Gonzalez and Lawrence Welsh; edited by Lisa McNiel; introduction by David Dorado Romo.
Description: First edition. | Albuquerque: University of New Mexico Press, 2018.
Identifiers: LCCN 2018001015 (print) | LCCN 2018006567 (e-book) | ISBN 9780826359018 (e-book) | ISBN 9780826359001 (pbk.: alk. paper)
Subjects: LCSH: Mexican-American Border Region—Pictorial works. | Literature and photography.
Classification: LCC F787 (e-book) | LCC F787 .C88 2018 (print) | DDC 972/.1—dc23
LC record available at https://lccn.loc.gov/2018001015

Cover photograph: Bruce Berman, De Soto. Arrey Derry, New Mexico, 2010.
Designed by Lisa C. Tremaine
Composed in ITC Officina

This publication is made possible in part by a generous contribution from El Paso Community College.

CONTENTS

Bruce Berman and Lawrence Welsh

EDITOR'S NOTE

Pairing these poems and photographs was easier and more difficult than first thought. As a native El Pasoan, the images resonated together for me in profoundly subjective and familiar ways, and I found myself occasionally doing audience analysis: Will an "outsider" get it? Are these two pieces together too obvious? Does it really matter if anyone gets it, and what is the "it," the resonance or dissonance that I want the observer/reader to get? And, despite the fact that for me these poems and photographs are home, am I really an "insider" at all? But the truth is that the work of connecting the photographs and poems did not present itself like a simple dichotomy or correspondence, just as the border itself transcends such classifications for those of us who exist here; or, if it is defined in those terms—"this side" or "that side," "both sides," "one side," "a line," "the bridge"—all of these designations exist at once on multiple levels.

The editorial process itself reflected this complexity. Initially, I received a group of Ray Gonzalez's poems already selected by Welsh and a group of Lawrence Welsh's poems already selected by Gonzalez. Then a separate group of photos culled by Bruce Berman arrived *after* he had read the Gonzalez/Welsh poems. In effect I had three distinct piles of poems and images that had been traversed by all three artists but not organized or remembered or experienced as a whole. My task was to pair poem and image—not match, but pair—and then to sequence the poems and images in a meaningful and almost rhythmic way, as one scores a script or piece of music.

Therefore, when I read the poems and absorbed both the word images and the photographic ones, they came together in unexpected ways that combined the lived experiences of this place called the border. The images are not just images. They are lives. People, not myths or academic theories. Individuals, not figures out of Old West romances. Changing frames of history and subjective time shape this place of literal and gritty metaphor where the actual scorpion of one's childhood experience is now also the rumored icon of a drug cartel, and so scorpion is both arachnid and war at once. Suddenly and almost subliminally, Gonzalez's poem "Looking for the Scorpion" finds itself next to Berman's photo of a *federale* with a gun stuck in his pants.

Such a blending of associations, both consciously and unconsciously, guided the pairing of poem and picture, at times obvious, at other times evocative, provoked by one word, image, title, and, to be honest, subjective memory. Welsh's poem "Dyer's Angels" references a street in El Paso, a straight shot to the Edge of Texas ranch and restaurant, past diners and hotel dives unchanged since the '50s with names like The Clock and The Royal Hawaiian. In its preserved decay along the way, Dyer may seem dire indeed. However, even for those unfamiliar with the street's local significance, Welsh's Dyer evokes the borderline itself, along with other highways, other paths disappearing into liminal horizons of unrealized promises, unlimited and limited by the road, the line itself. Similarly, the border is localized and generalized at once. The border is accessible and inaccessible, and as Pablo Vila points out in his ethnography, crossing borders enigmatically reinforces them through this very act of recognition.

Berman, Gonzalez, and Welsh capture this suspended intersection of connectedness and separation without judgment or apology, especially without the dualities I have inadvertently set up here. Their clarity of vision, where images breathe and bleed, where place is personal, and where tortillas do authentically exist beyond ethnic stereotypes, allows us to break through the line and see combinations in new and startling ways.

LISA MCNIEL

INTRODUCTION

The border has become a ubiquitous metaphor, a blurred line, a run-on sentence that means everything and nothing. Ironically, the more concrete, real, and militarized the actual borderline between Mexico and the United States has become, the more it has been dematerialized in the literary imagination. But this isn't necessarily a bad thing. It's understandable why smashing through borders, all kinds of borders, would be a powerful trope today. Indeed, how *do* we cut through that barbed-wire fence that runs right down the middle of our minds?

Cutting the Wire, a masterful collaboration between photographer Bruce Berman and poets Ray Gonzalez and Lawrence Welsh, offers us a way to look again, to *really* look, at this part of the world that the metaphors are based on. Berman, who has photographed and lived in El Paso for more than four decades, sees himself as a documentarian who uses his camera to record what's in front of him rather than for, as he puts it, "mere self-expression." In this regard, his life's work follows in a long tradition of documentarian photographers who have shot along the El Paso–Juárez border in the last century including Russell Lee, Dorothea Lange, Samuel Tinoco, and Otis Aultman. Berman's visual investigations, firmly grounded on everyday realities and the spaces of the border—detention centers, smeltertown cemeteries, kids playing along a river levee, crosses on telephone posts for the disappeared—are exactly the stuff the poetry of Gonzalez and Welsh is made of. Their poems often revisit some of the very same terrains from which previous authors such as William Carlos Williams, Oscar Zeta Acosta, Ricardo Sanchez, and Cormac McCarthy have drawn their inspiration.

Ray Gonzalez's travels through the streets, buildings, and landmarks of the border serve as the bedrock for his exploration of what *fronteriza* writer Gloria Anzaldúa called the "geographies of the soul." Gonzalez writes,

I return to El Paso often.
It must be the river and the cross on the peak.

In my father's house, a strange woman.

and

Another dreaded hometown dream
where everything has changed
and the buildings you fear entering
might set off a nightmare to wake you.

El Paso is inhabited by family ghosts, desert dragons, and other visitations from the past. In his poem "Home Town," Gonzalez summons recent, distant, and invented memories only to make them suddenly vanish.

Remember who
smashed the pickup and got away?
A mountain lion wandered into downtown
El Paso and was immediately shot dead.
When Pancho Villa entered the town, he hid in
a grand hotel and watched his mistress undress.

[. . .]

In 1929, a newspaper boy selling the *Herald Post*
on Paisano and Santa Fe went up in flames,
witnesses claiming spontaneous combustion.
The boy simply ignited and went away.

The multilayered histories of the border landscape provide an inexhaustible supply of rich and fertile raw material for both Gonzalez and Welsh. But their poetic visions allow them to capture elements of a personal and collective past that historians have often failed to record.

In "After the Sons of Villa," Welsh describes a group of migrant workers who have just returned from a *pisca* in the sweltering fields:

god please watch over these men and women
as they pack up and slip into the back rooms of red light
let them take on stillness for black leather

white stetson hats that shade the 107 degree heat
their eyes protected from the blistering sun, sand and names
that will own the avenue
become its pitch and the essence that they were here forever
and never really there for the historians to see

Seeing what others fail to see is a recurrent theme in Welsh's poems. He looks closely at the tracks left behind by those who break through borders in search of opportunities and new beginnings. Welsh writes,

hidden by the river
in creosote, chamisa
the border patrol never sees
or the federal boundary authority
with binoculars
for chihuahua's best slip across

[. . .]

i see a mirage
or shadows kneeling
their eyes and hands
pointing only
to the sun

Cutting the Wire is in many ways a deeply spiritual book. Berman recently decided to shoot only in black and white because he believes it is the best means to capture what he calls the "grim reality of the border." Yet flickers of light and a subdued aura of dignity emanate even from his darkest photographs. Similarly pervasive in Gonzalez's and Welsh's poems is a search for moments of illumination and traces of the sublime in places where few would look.

Their poetry reminds us that to cut through the line we must first examine the barbed wire itself very closely and only afterward look beyond to what is on the other side.

DAVID DORADO ROMO

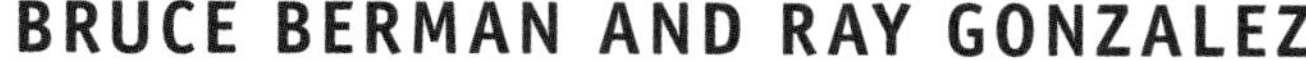

BRUCE BERMAN AND RAY GONZALEZ

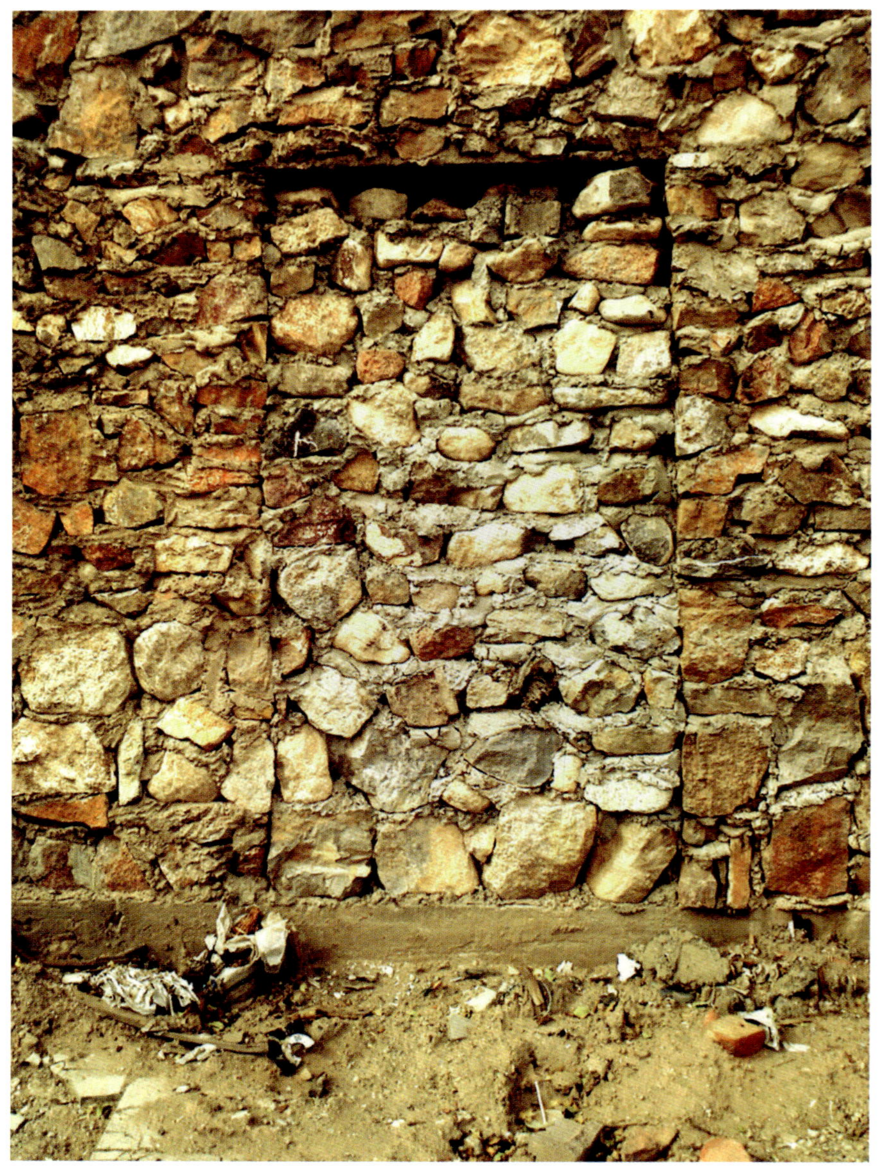

Filled-in door. El Paso, Texas, 2012.

It Should Have Happened Long Ago

I return to El Paso often.
It must be the river and the cross on the peak.

The sun withers in clouds like men careful
in stepping through the back door.

I remove the stone step.
In my father's house, a strange woman.

Inside my mother's walls, a white sheet,
and a globe of the earth in a photograph.

Let those who favor mystery speak.
It is the stone step where a boy fell.

In my home, books collect dust.
On the mountain wall, a painted red hand.

El Paso

You have another dreaded hometown dream where everything has changed and the buildings you fear entering might set off a nightmare to wake you. This time, the streets are brilliant and your grandmother's ghost walks with you downtown. You cross the main street and stare at tall buildings that weren't there when you were growing up, your invisible grandmother following you as you cross to San Jacinto Plaza. Instead of the fountain where they kept alligators, there are old men in sombreros taking a siesta under the trees. You are disappointed because it is the midday nap of stereotype, the poor Mexicans doing nothing but sleeping. "I thought everything had changed," you mumble in your sleep. Your grandmother gives the men fresh stacks of home-made tortillas, masa patted and cooked on her stove in her house, the flames the same fire that appears each time you dream, the old men in their sombreros waking up to eat and stare at you. Each one shakes his head at you as your grandmother disappears beyond the river where a town of empty houses waits for her, but that is not part of your dream.

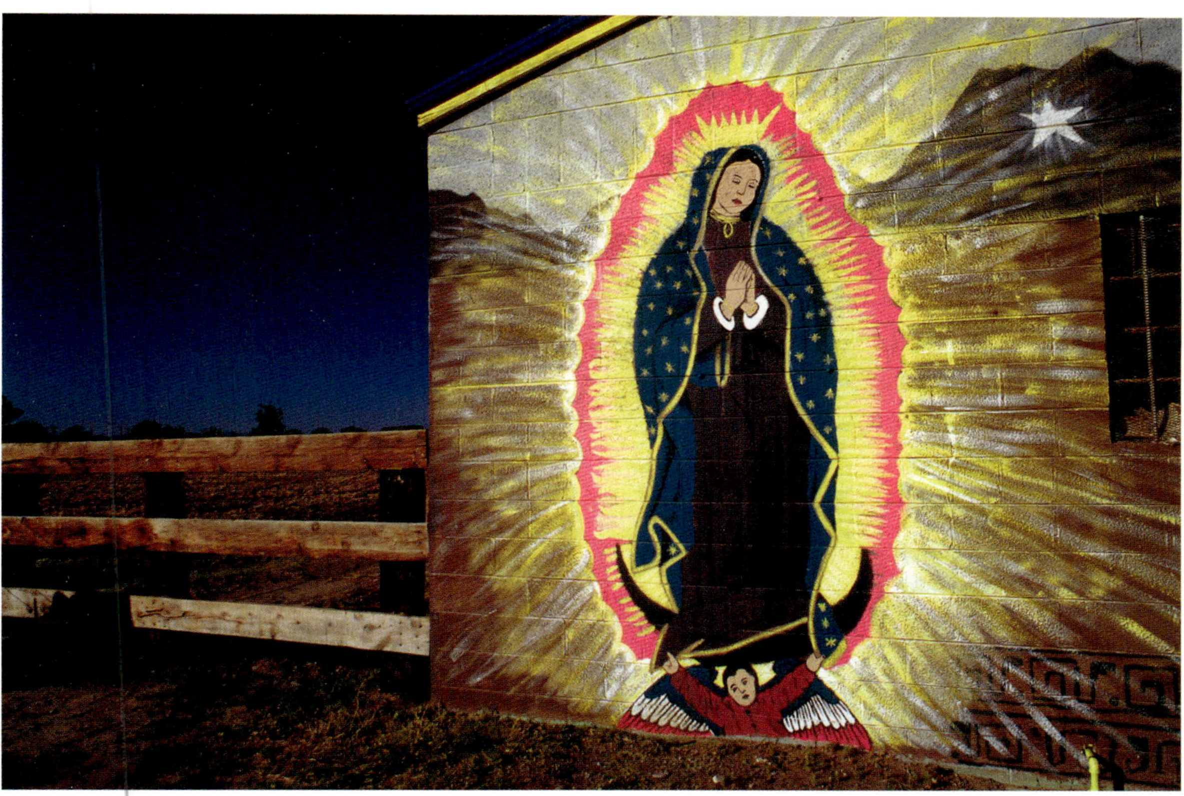

Guadalupe #5. Lower Valley, El Paso, Texas, 2003.

The Fingers Light the Western Stars

The Milky Way was crossed by
a streaking satellite on its path
beyond Ursa Major, the galaxy
above the cemetery at Cloride,
where graves hold families killed
by Apaches in the Gila, the great
Andromeda constellation Kenneth
Rexroth worshipped vanishing
beyond the mountains above
the mining town.

The last time I climbed here,
Mr. Clarke was ninety-eight years old, toothless
and proud, the last survivor of a Cloride
mining family, his parents killed by
a tribe, their bodies taken to punish
him for staying alive.

The cemetery protects its names
as it releases distant planets that
are treeless as they go by in sleep,
names in the sky draping myths
around my intrusion, pines and
salt cedars covering the path.

There were clusters of stars
Mr. Clarke couldn't see when
we looked up and guessed.
He pointed at constellations that
he said never lie, the old man
wheezing to death three years later,
becoming the light in space
that falls in the desert each time
the stars are correctly identified.

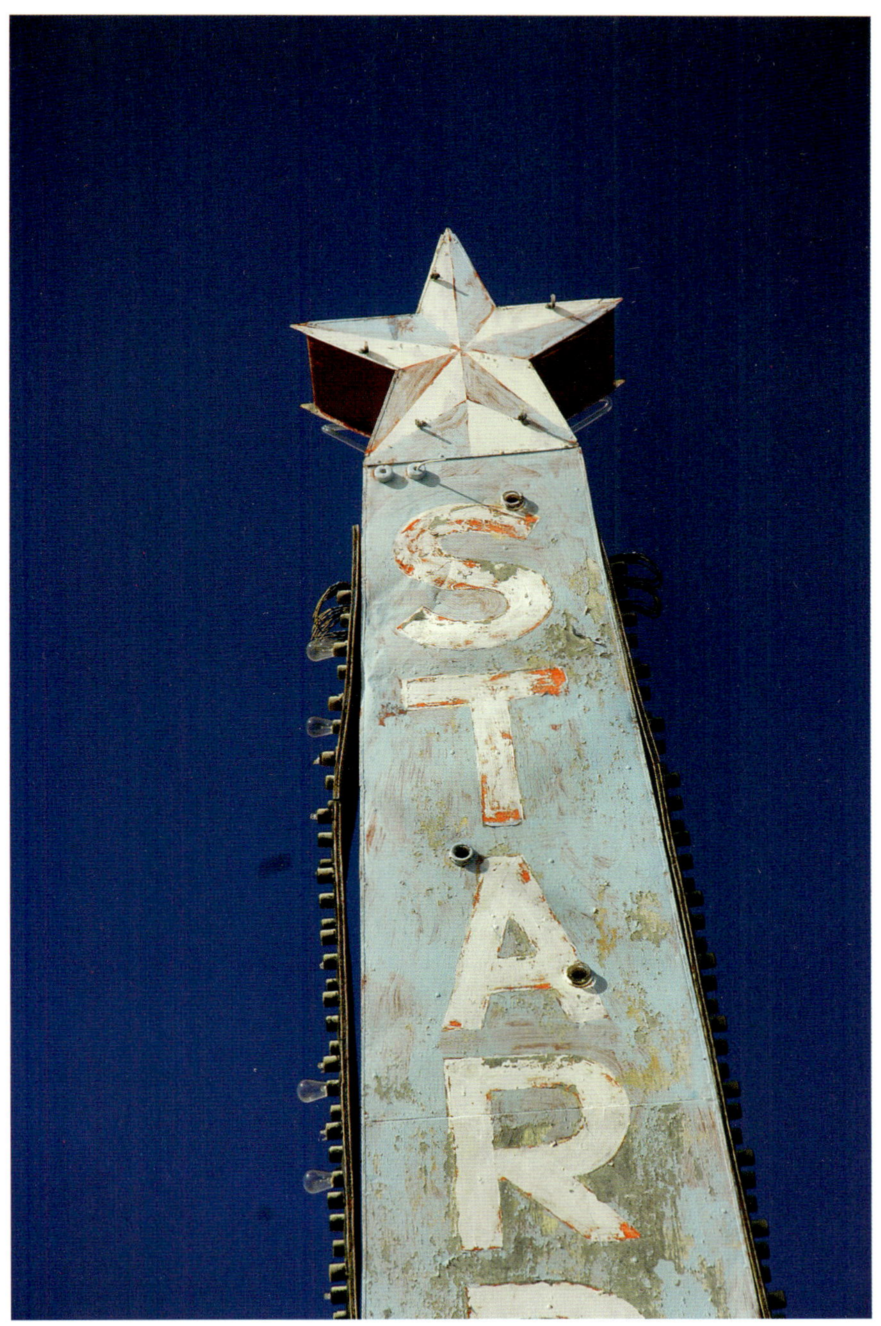

The Star of Marfa. Marfa, Texas, 2007.

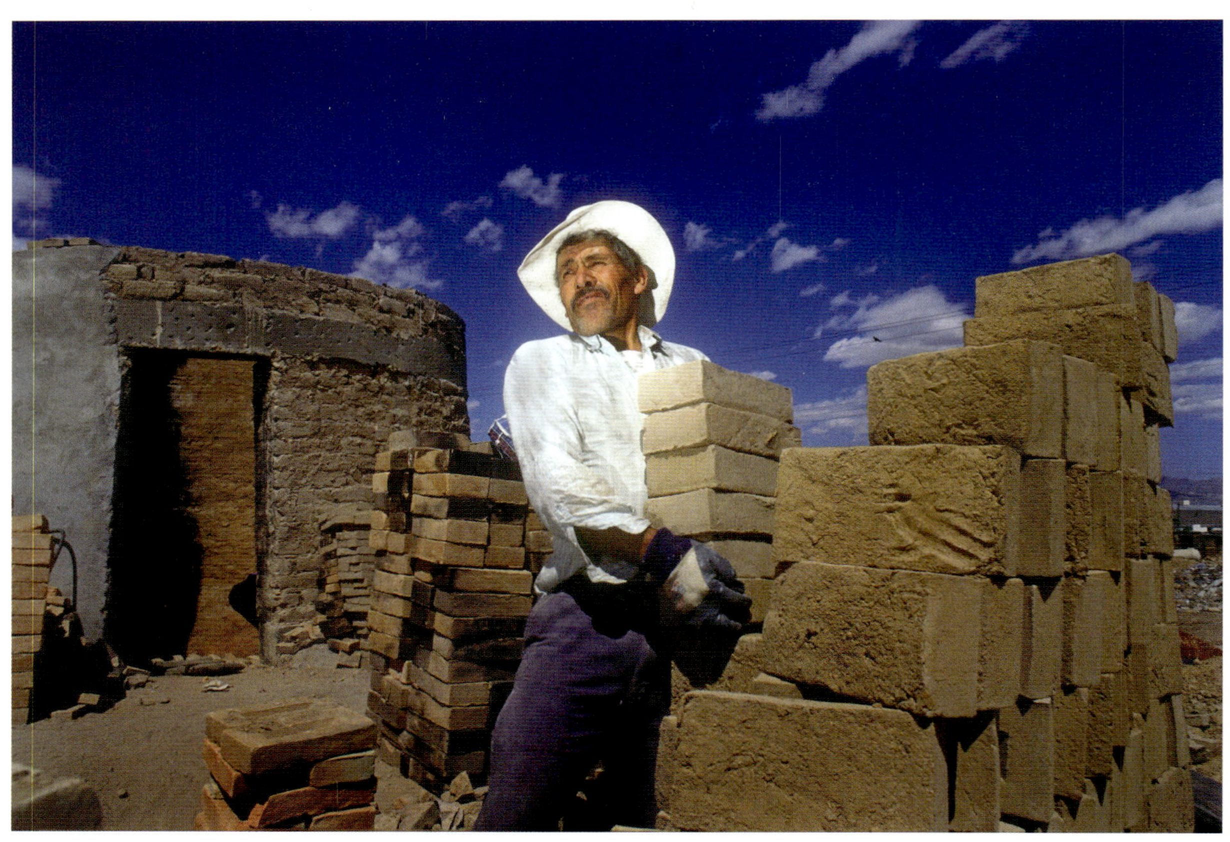

The Brickmaker / El Ladrillero. Juárez, Mexico, 1986.

Under the Adobe

The Apaches of southern Arizona
believed the desert was full of dragons.

A creation myth gave them permission
to turn them into rattlesnakes.

For a few of the people,
stones were living seeds,

their hands clutching them
to signal under the junipers,

the dragons burning the mountains
each night to find water hidden there,

the thirsty people dropping the stones,
their circle calling the rattlers to come.

In My Hands

I discover the mountain range
resembling the spine buried
where I never stepped,
bones hidden to make me
guess how desire gets from
here to there, the rope of
thorns bleeding to warn me
what I pull out of the marker
is cutting into what can never
be named in the wilderness.

In my hands, I hold
the thorns that fell out
of the monument at Otros Peak,
sharp vines twisted around
the dry blossoms as if something
grew inside the historic concrete
without becoming flowers.

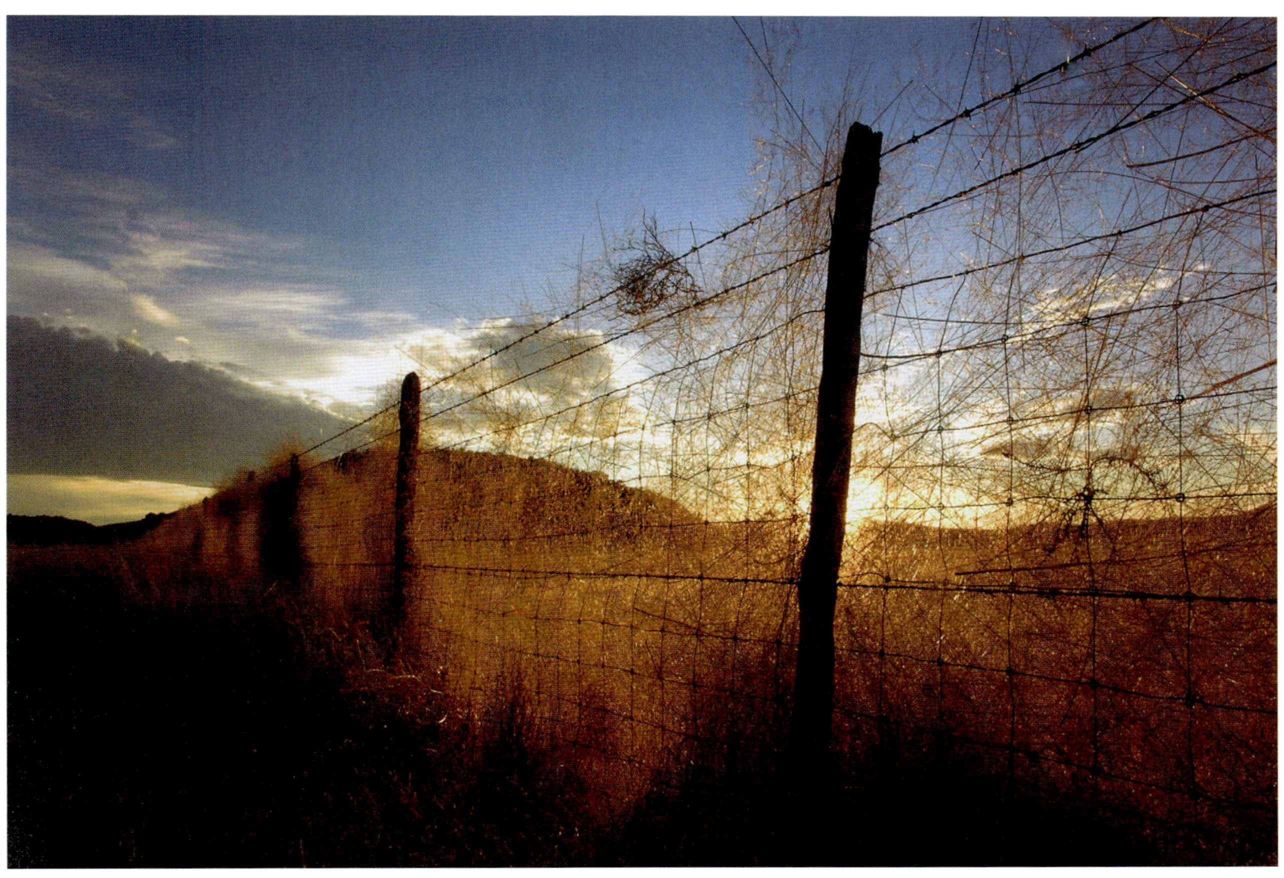

West Texas Sunset. 2006.

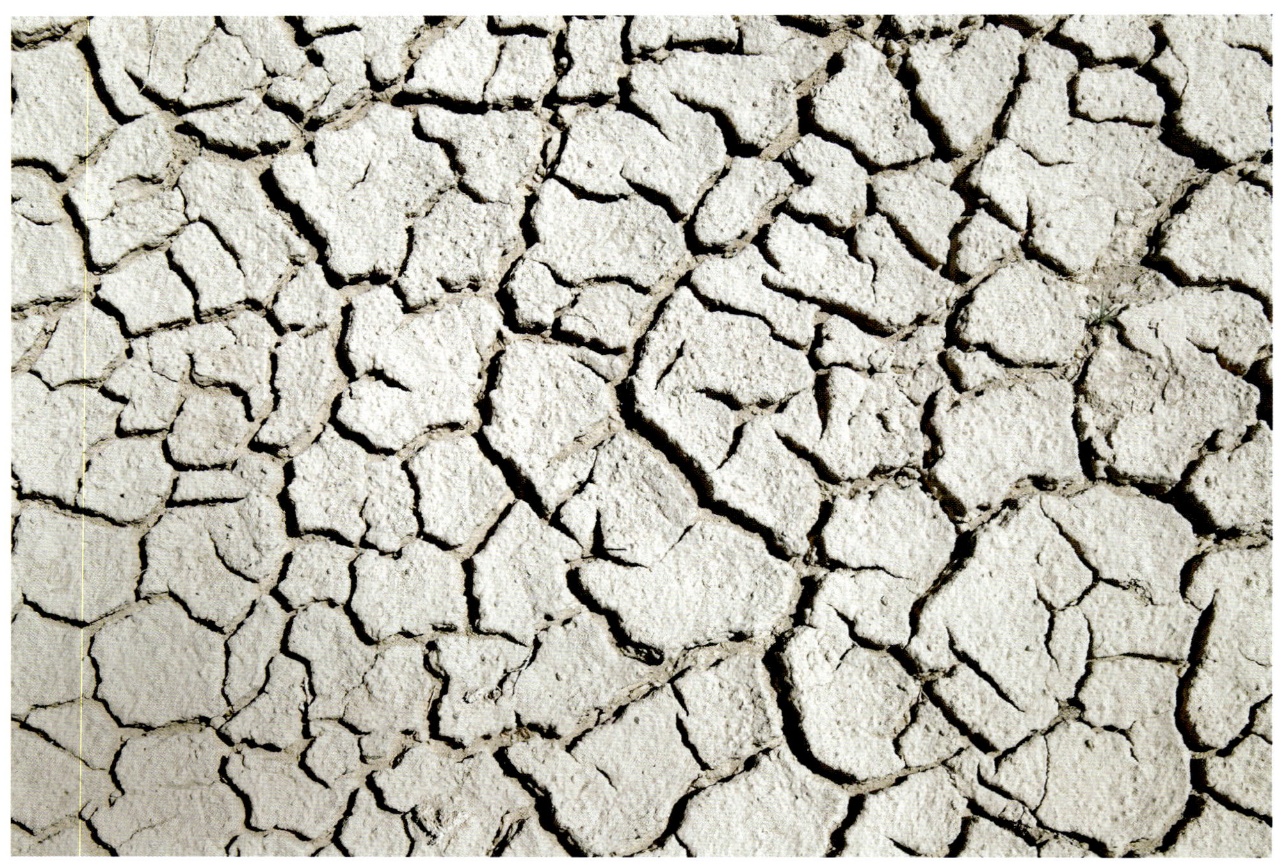

Cracked Earth. Highway 60, New Mexico, 2010.

The Desert Floor

The desert floor burns the legend
and erodes what I believe.

I cross the plain as if weight on
the back of a walking man will

disappear in the sweat.
The desert floor is not flat.

It contains fragmented ground
where I come upon the saguaro,

talk to my grandfather who rode
the trains through the Sonora,

descending to the arroyo to warn me
the boy who crosses the desert

is the man who never leaves home
because dust storms clear the mind.

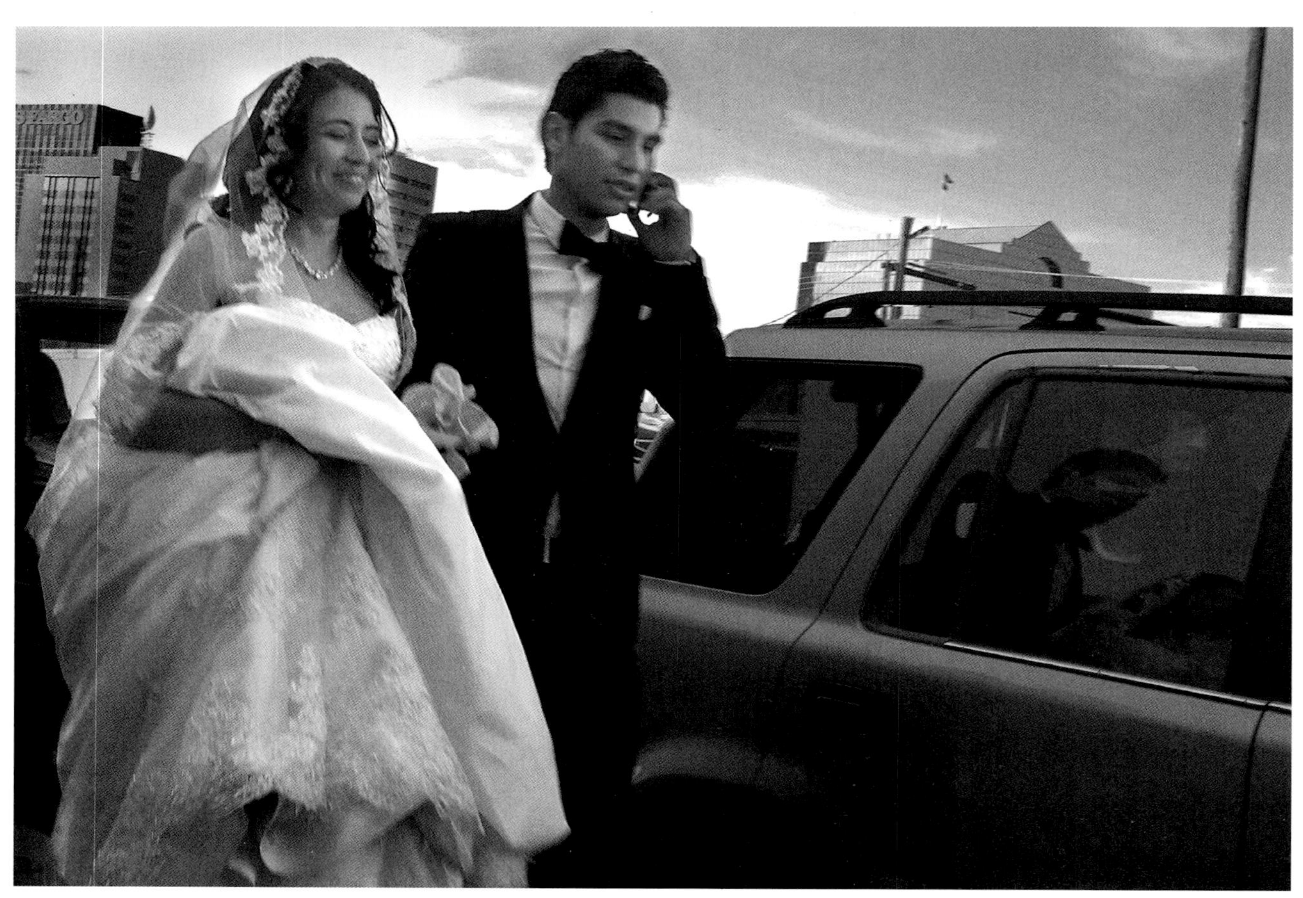

Southside Wedding. El Paso, Texas, 2001.

Footprints

Feet are erased by desert
winds that rearrange large and
small tracks, worn shoes and
blistered toes, even triangles
the sidewinder carves as
a warning in the geometric dirt.

A pair moves across the line
as if the body had wings,
its leap to the other side leaving
clues to an old trick outdated
by power lines.

The feet lead to paradise
with hope walking this far.
Footprints disappear at the wall,
never to be seen again,
though sandals are there,
stolen to leave bloody
patterns in the dirt.

There are footprints of thirsty
children with a hurt woman,
even the mark of the one-legged
man who survived the massacre
to gain the sands of the earth.

Black Border Wall

Secretly, the men cross the river, the sun
at their backs carving a face on the mountain.

The men's hands are bleeding, trails of sun
illuminating the road that ends at the border

wall where the Cristo Rey sun brands faces on
the black surface, heat steaming off the steel,

vanishing across sand dunes that blow each
time headlights move and vans get full.

The wall follows the cameras mounted on
poles, miles of unfinished wall rising higher

than the electric eye that can't photograph
the hidden face of their God.

The men wish the wall was finished so
they would have two choices—turn back

or leave their loved ones on their own,
the torn entrance letting them slide down

to the ground where women and children
wait for the hot night to bring them water.

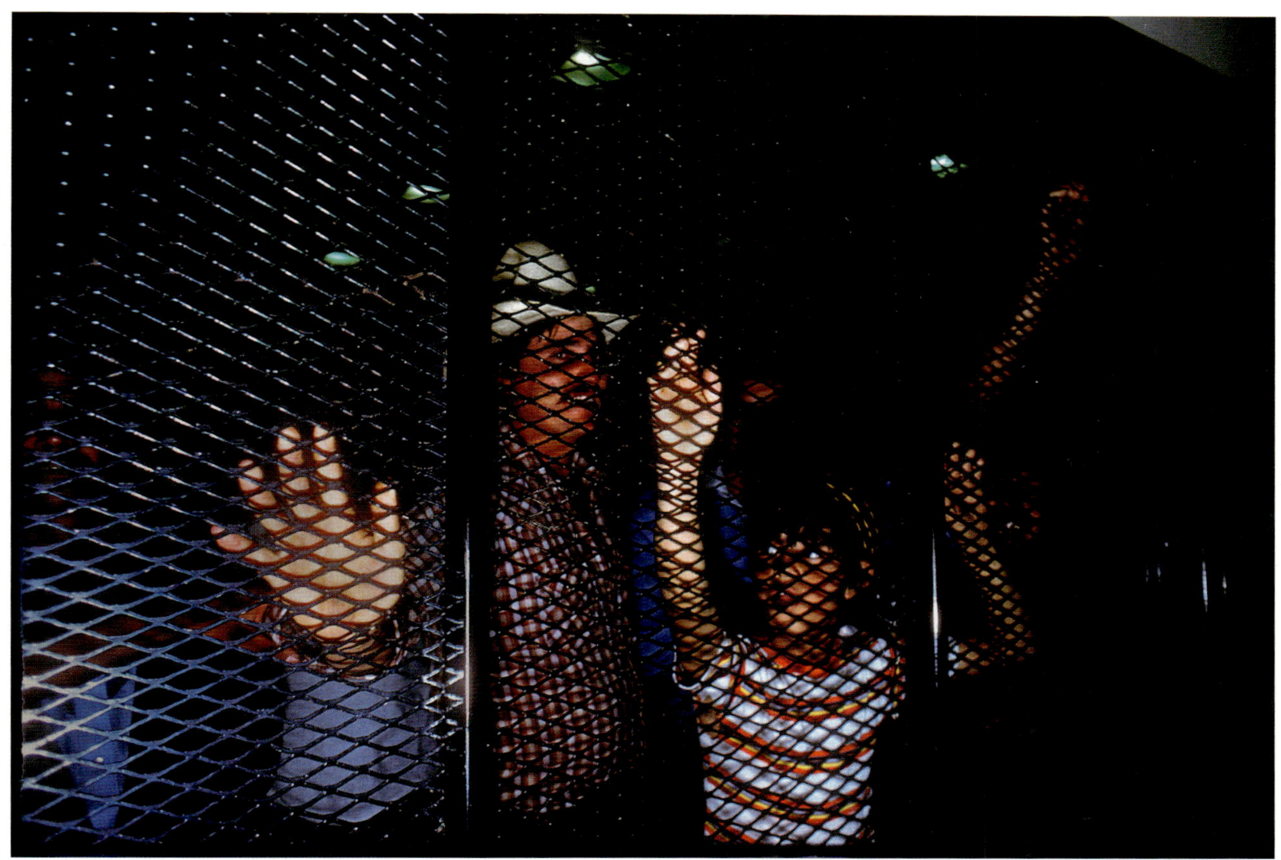

Detention cell. Paso del Norte Bridge, El Paso, Texas, 1984.

Distance

Do not stare at the Organ Peaks.
They sharpen the sky in patterns
you are unable to decipher.

Do not cross the Rio Grande often,
because it is a ritual lost in the ruins
at Mountain Air long ago.

Descending the stone stairs at Abo,
you felt it in your chest.
When you stared into the kiva there,

weeds growing on its floor trembled
and the falling rock kept you safe.
Do not visit again and pretend

you are part of the mountain,
because the desert will carve
symbols on your sunburned back.

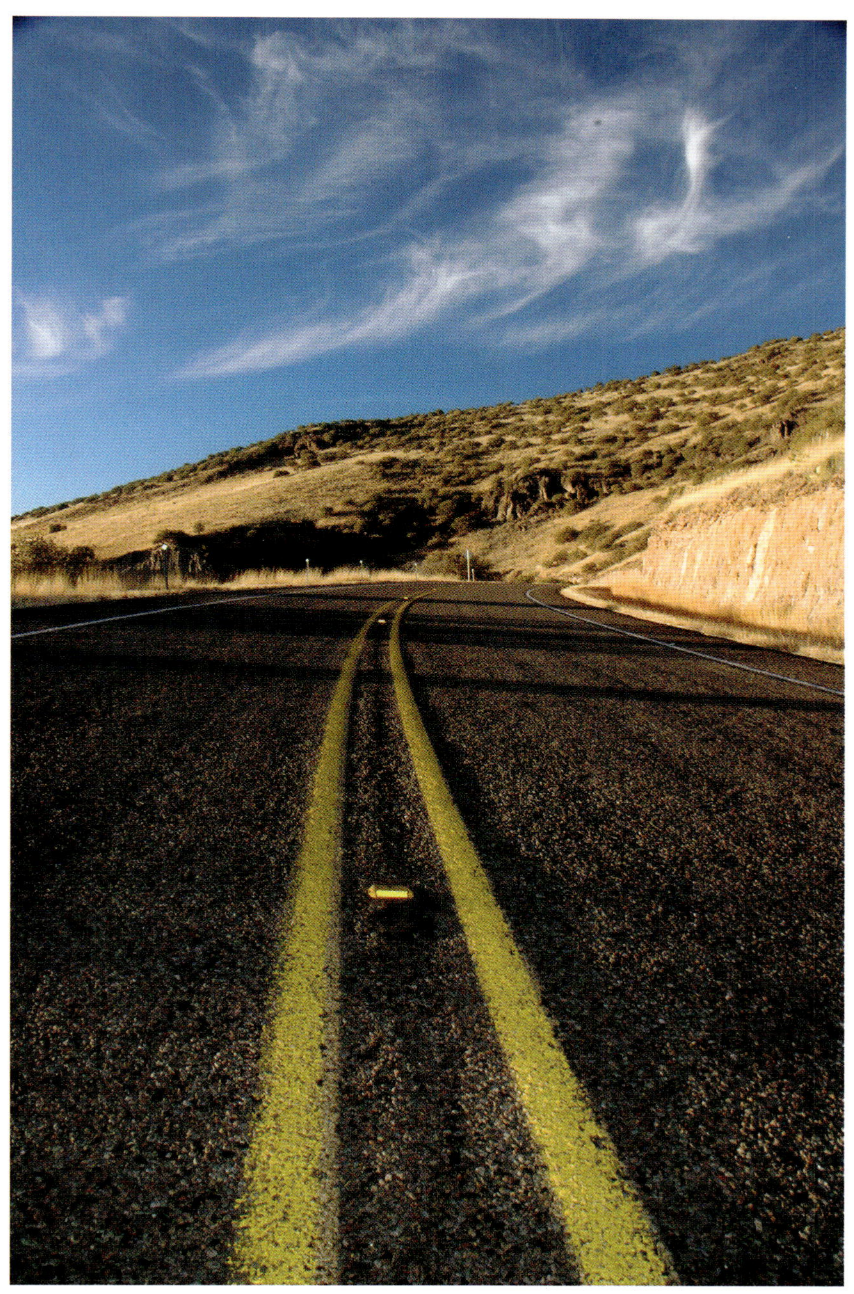

West Texas Highway. 2007.

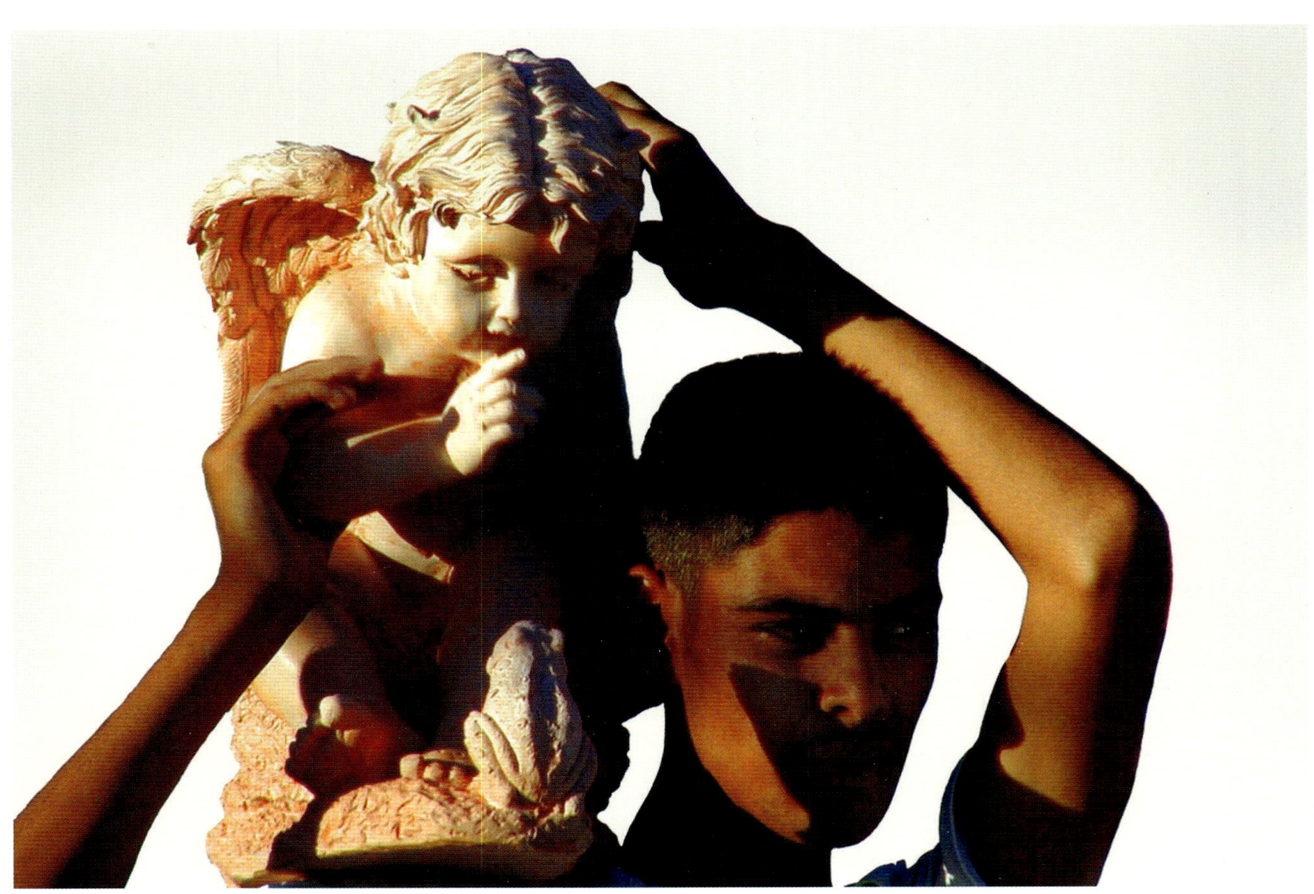

Angel of Juárez. Juárez, Mexico, 1999.

It Flew Away

Image of hands inside the clay jar
with mud dripping beyond attention
and a design where strange figures
are bent over, the vanishing advice
stolen by a prophet and hidden inside
a conception vessel where the circle
dance is painted on the walls of
the mind where the event took place
without the thinker being aware that

the story is fire intended to reveal
how the mouth contains the object
until the string of beads reaches
the stomach, the eater swallowing
to prove that those possessed are
blessed from within and not from
above, the photograph an attempt

to unveil what it means, when it was
taken, and how easily the figure in
the background resembles a ghost
that is not supposed to be there,
preserved by hands inside the clay jar,
parchment papers on the rack drying
until the text is translated by someone
who speaks the language.

T-Shirt Shop on Santa Fe Street

I almost bought a T-shirt with
Pancho Villa's face on it,

the bandido pointing a finger,
"Ese, Gringo! I want you!"

His huge moustache and sombrero
would be perfect for Minnesota.

They didn't have my size so I almost
bought the famous Che Guevara face,

revolution alive and well on the border,
but I had worn that years ago.

I found La Virgen de Guadalupe
on a green T-shirt, perfect size,

but I hesitated because I couldn't
wear her on my chest, candles of

recent mourning holding me back.
I bought a soccer T-shirt, the sport

big down there, this team claiming
a rhinoceros for a mascot, the image

rather small, though its horn raged
across my stomach as I tried it on,

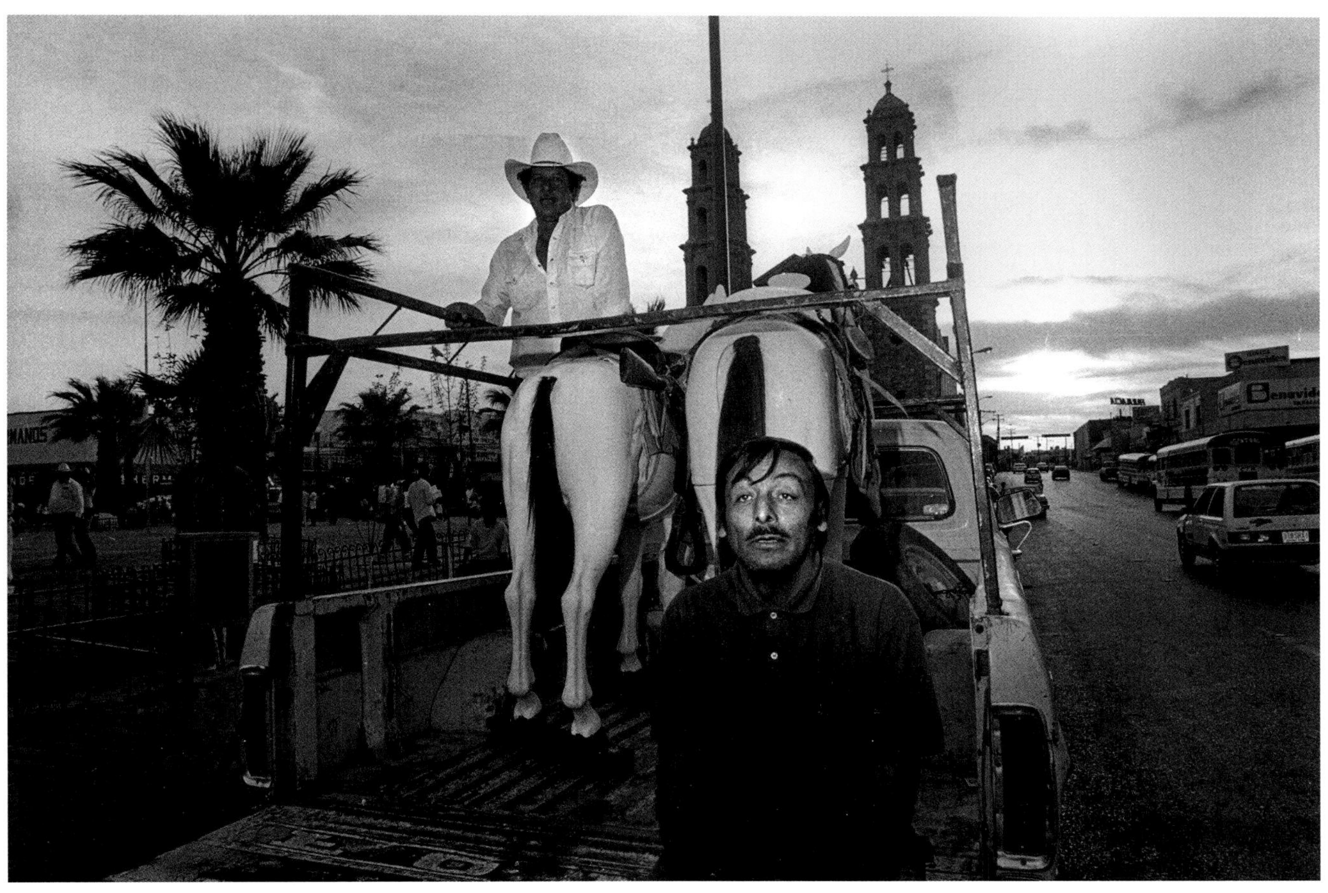

Tired man with ponies. Juárez, Mexico, 1997.

wished Pancho Villa had been there
to warn me the animal that rages

is the creature that chooses us
when other T-shirt sizes are wrong.

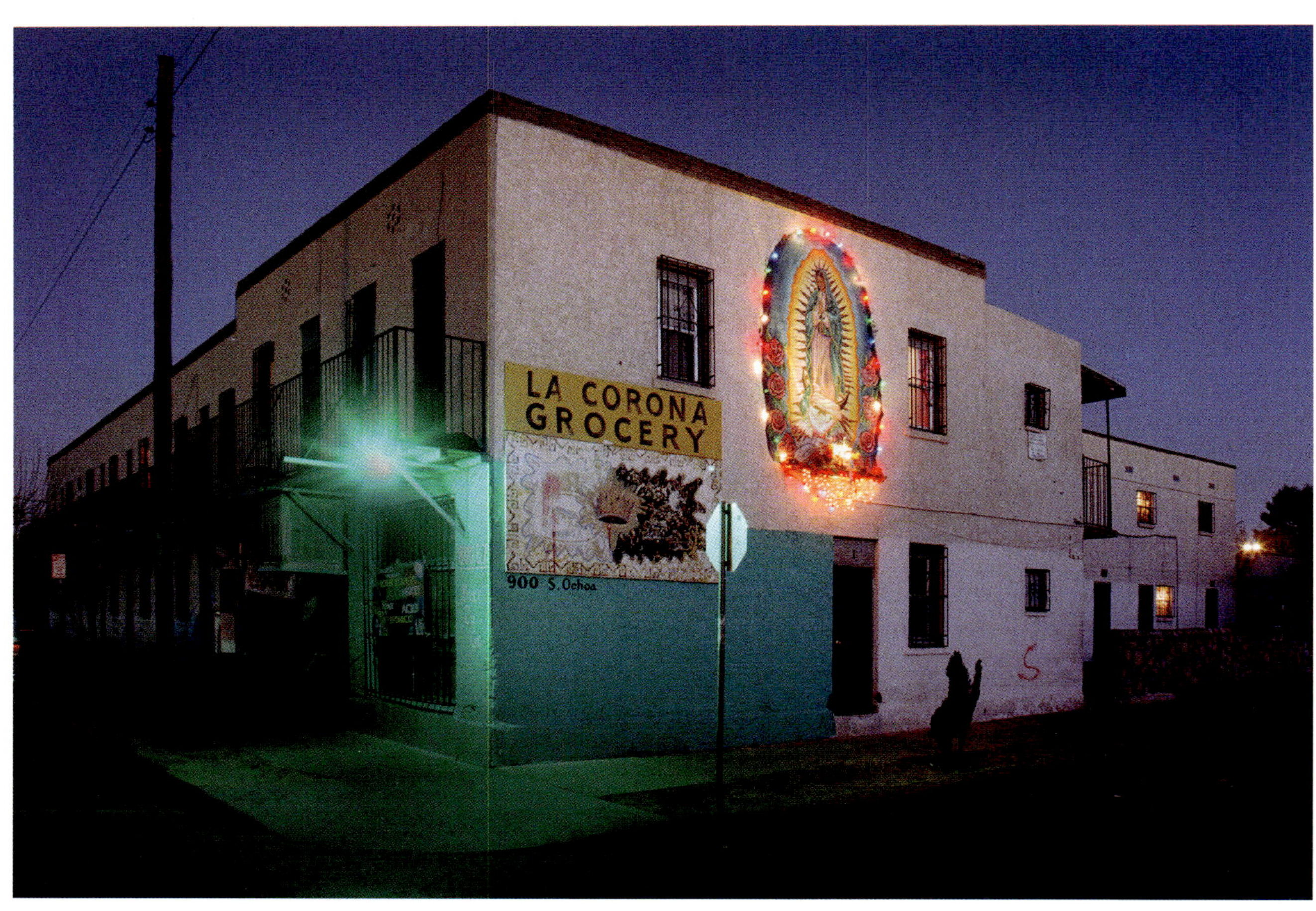

La Corona. Segundo Barrio, El Paso, Texas, 2005.

Tortilla Factory

1
Sometimes walking late at night,
I stop before the tortilla factory,

knowing the masa must be late
if the fire still glows inside.

I smell the aroma of things that
have not happened in a long time.

There is a crucifix on one wall,
its black cross marking the spot

where ashes drifted down
and business went on,

the light in the factory window
blinking off and on.

When the morning trucks arrive
to take the fresh tortillas away,

they find me hungry
and waving.

2
Ghost grandmothers bake them,
though I was told not to write about

abuelas because I need
to outgrow my ethnicity,
the need to show how ethnic life was.

Faces appear on tortillas
as secret codes of love and death

between the maker of the masa
and the boy who ate them,

brown lines on the tortilla rearranging
themselves off the stove.

Childhood stuffed me with fattening
tortillas and beans, and I am
not to share details because
    stereotypes
are hotter than the jalapeños I bite
    into.

If the stove is left on, I might scorch
my hands, though she never burned

a tortilla, and I had to imagine the day
she would, so I could grab the black

tortilla and run out the kitchen door
with ashes for her grave.

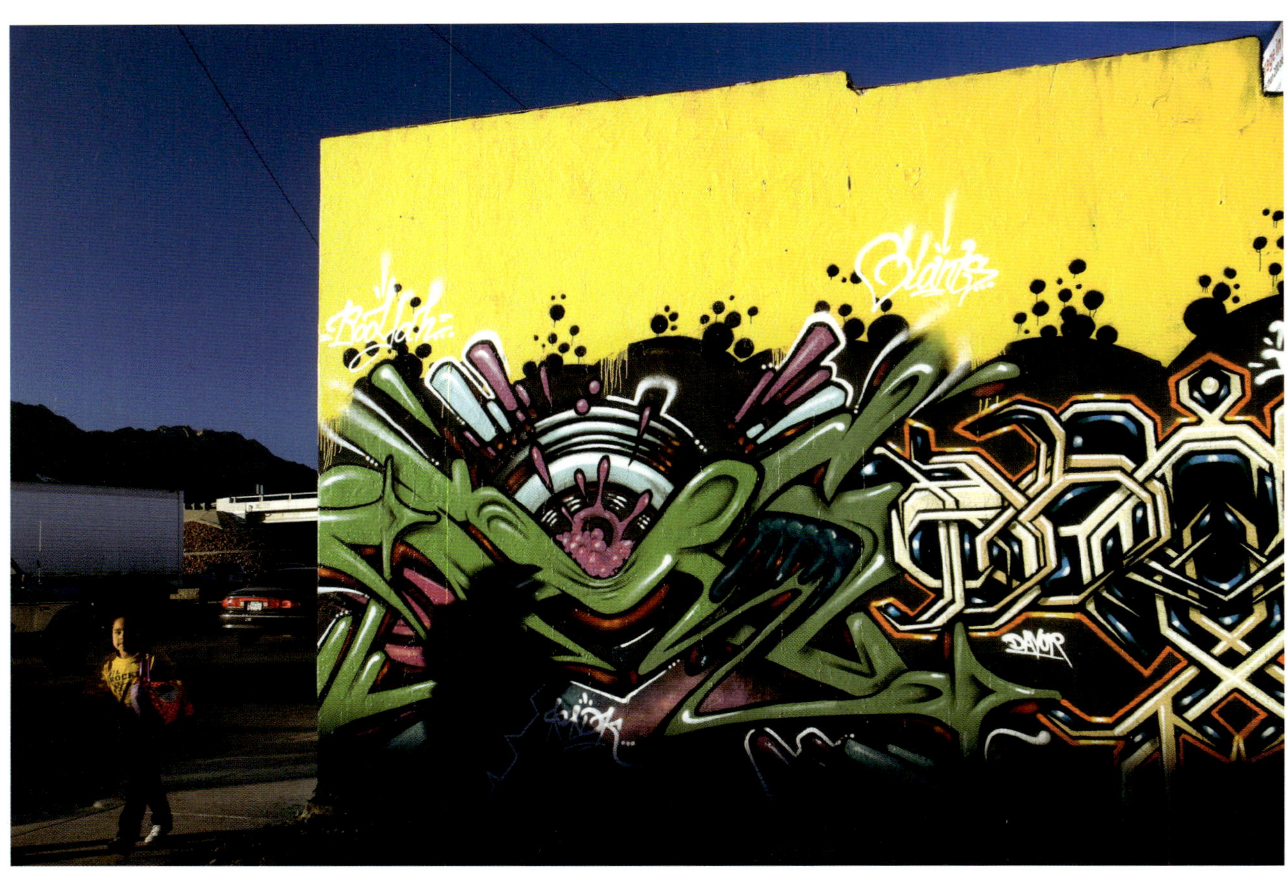

School kid heading home to Juárez. El Paso, Texas, 2007.

The Visitations on Alameda Street

I approach the visitations
as I walk down Alameda,
my attention bound in poverty,
wired economies pushing the poor
to sit down and weep.

I dwell in the visitations, my need
to live in the interstices of the clock
a way of easing into the vapor of
my city, its empty blocks chiseled
in graffiti concrete that reveals
figures blessing me with chips of
asphalt from the empty street.

I surrender to the Sunday morning
mass where the feathered owl
watches the road for worshippers,
its three heavens becoming two
when I emerge to discover its
silence is clawed into the tree when
the last visitation recognizes me.

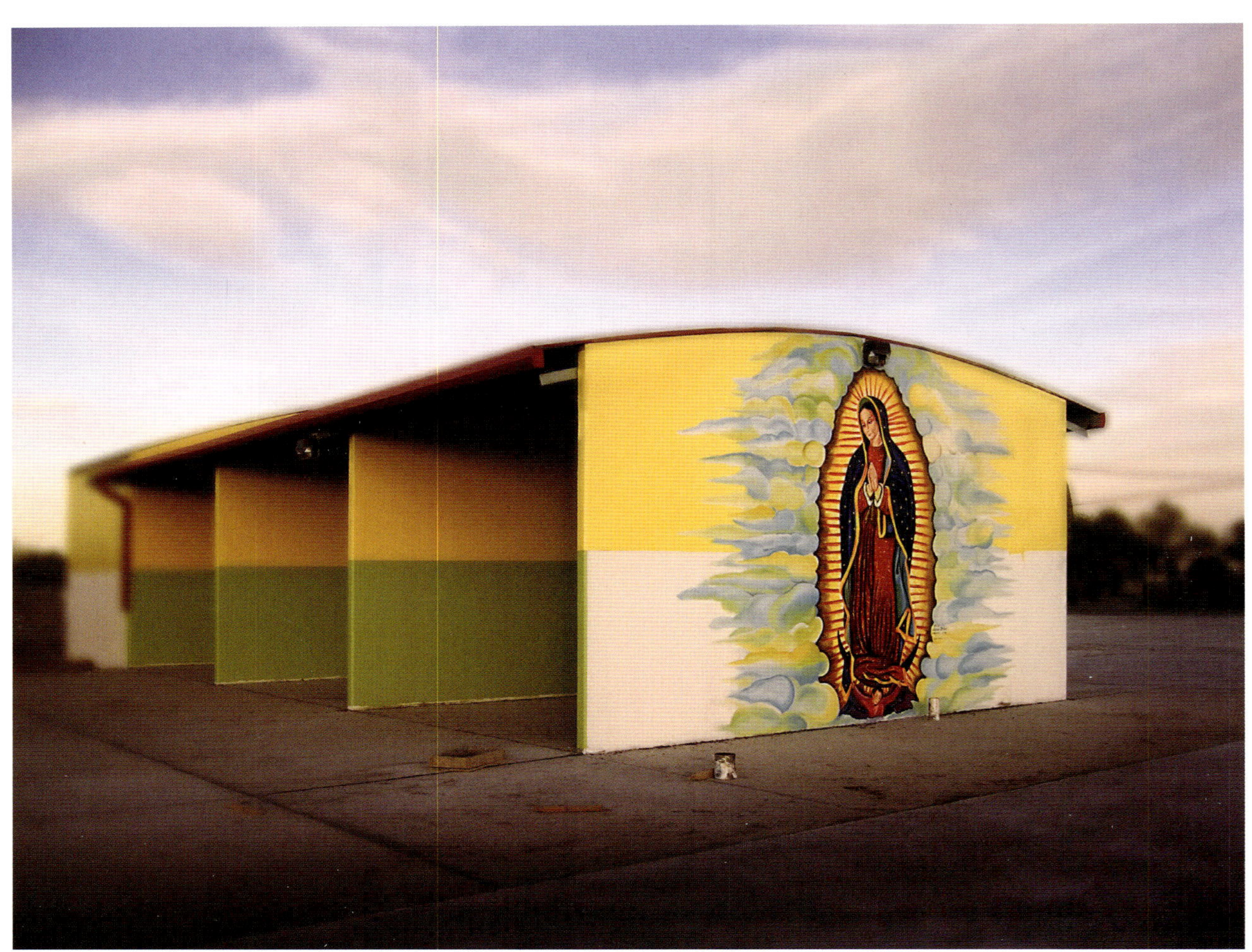

The Virgin's Car Wash. El Paso, Texas, 2006.

Home Town

If I quit writing about El Paso, would
the Chihuahua desert remain in upheaval?
Would historic buildings rise after being
torn down in a desert that never ages?
Concordia Cemetery might return my
grandparents or my father's family
who never let me be.
My grandmother Julia's house, where
I was born, was left standing after
the freeway was built.
The 2006 flood erased nostalgia,
making me reread her books of mud
etched in brown walls that disappeared.

If I quit walking Paisano and Texas Streets,
would childhood friends stumble out of cantinas
to wonder where I've been? Remember who
smashed the pickup and got away?
A mountain lion wandered into downtown
El Paso and was immediately shot dead.
When Pancho Villa entered the town, he hid in
a grand hotel and watched his mistress undress.
He took Juárez in 1914, stray bullets killing a few
El Pasoans watching the battle atop railroad cars.

What if the tortilla factory on Piedras never burned?
Would its chile burritos fill my Grandfather
Bonifacio who worked Arizona railroads after
fleeing Villa's men? They held the fourteen-year-old
conscript in a locked pen until he jumped

the fence and crossed the river.
In 1929, a newspaper boy selling the *Herald Post*
on Paisano and Santa Fe went up in flames,
witnesses claiming spontaneous combustion.
The boy simply ignited and went away.

If I quit writing, would violence end in Juárez,
its victims buried in the desert?
This is not about mountains and canyons—
it is about finding a border that carries my name
when I enter the city from the sky, the plane
descending over sunken lava craters,
gliding over new highways cutting the desert,
giving me time to map the fact I have never
been gone because this is not my house—
It is my home.

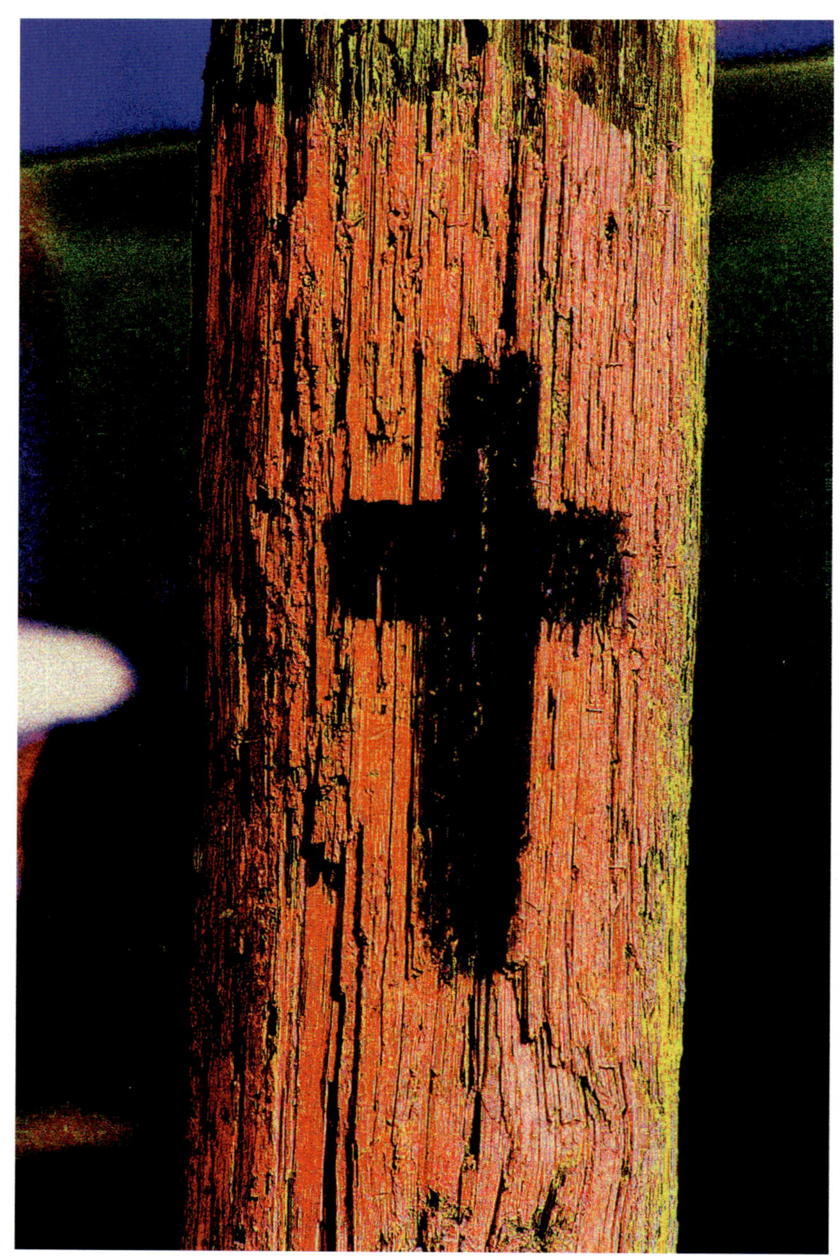

Black cross for the Desesparados. Juárez, Mexico, 2001.

Wood

I was hiking in the desert, and the rain
pushed me to the edge of the cut in the earth.

I pondered climbing down there when
I spotted something. I descended to find

it was a lizard perched on a high rock
in the arroyo, the sudden rainstorm leaving

a shallow stream at the bottom.
I descended carefully and threw a rock at it

before I saw it was made of wood,
a long-tailed reptile carved and left there

to stare at anyone entering the canyon.
I paused and looked around, wondering

if the artist was hiding down there,
the wooden lizard whittled into

fine detail, its scaly back and sharp head
staring at the sun as if something had

to happen to make it shudder and move.
I stood there for minutes and studied

the wooden lizard, then turned around
and slowly climbed out of the muddy

earth when it started raining again.

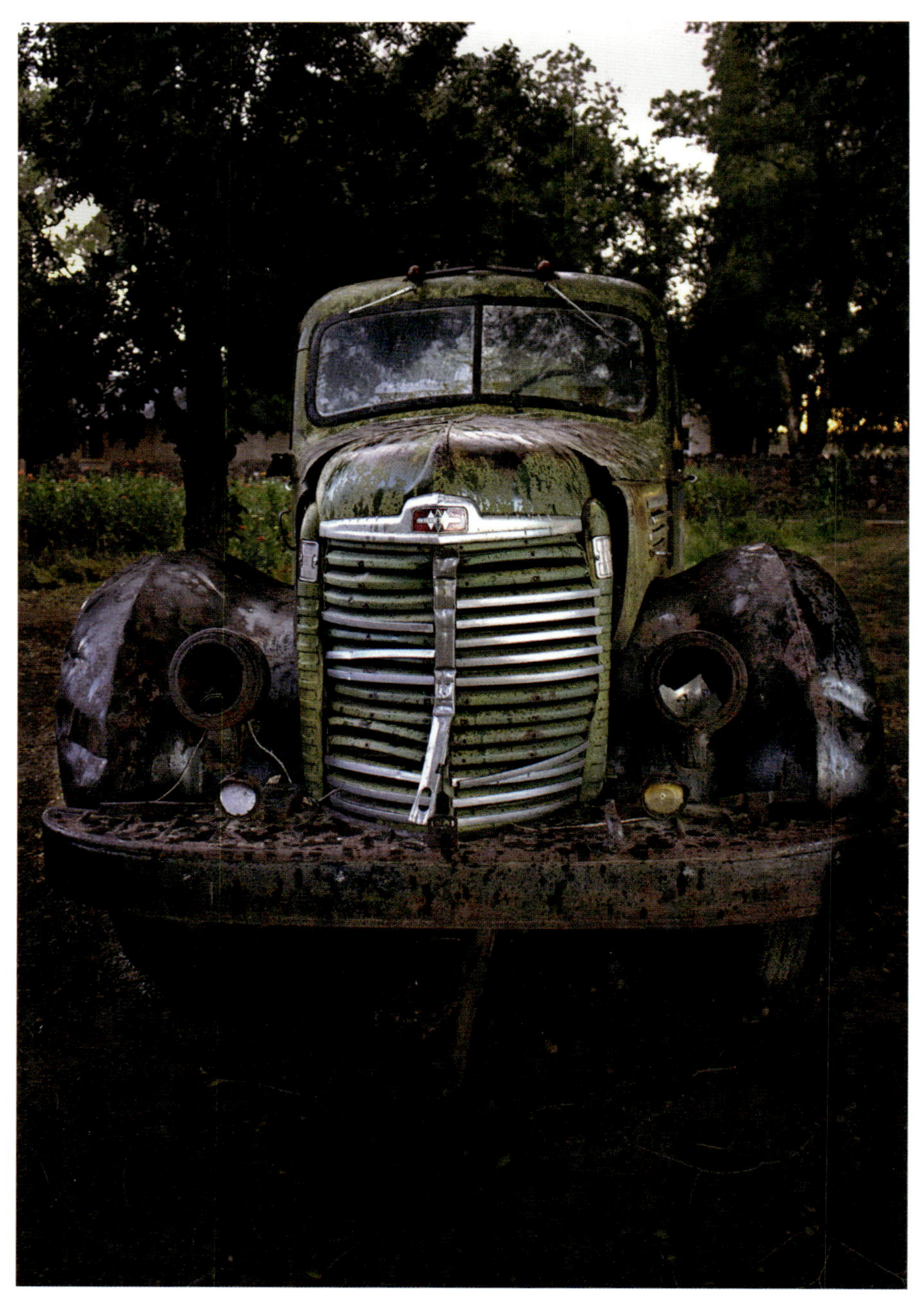

International Harvester. Mesilla Valley, 2017.

Chamberino

The blue river was a game in the mind,
the empty village touching the horizon.

When I stepped into the yard,
an empty basket swayed in the wind.

I took it off the clothesline and picked
slices of dry cactus off the ground.

When the basket was full, I paused.
Suddenly, the white tower of the church

blinded me, though I made it inside
and groped along the walls.

When I could see again, the river had
changed course and the bridge had collapsed,

an old tractor rusting in the field as crows
lit the fence with a vicious gathering.

Resler Canyon

Digging the mud fort as a boy, I fell
into the arroyo and lay stunned until
my father found me and dragged me up,
pulling off his leather belt to teach me
the wilderness is always there.
The back fence of our house overlooked
what is named Resler Canyon fifty years later.
It used to be a washed-out arroyo formed
after desert floods, raging water coming
out of drainage pipes from the highway,
not a single tree, deer, or rattler in the heat
where I roamed curious, mesquite bushes
dotting the hilly emptiness.

When I played there as an eight-year-old,
I chased lizards and listened to imaginary
rattles that never struck, my terrain preserved
for tomorrow by men and women who
chose the trail that ran from my high
school to my home, willed it as sacred space.
They needed to save something from
the past that was nothing but cactus,
my gym shoes and notebooks from
algebra class I dropped there.

My dirt fort must be somewhere in
the arroyo, conservationists making sure
El Pasoans don't forget arroyos of youth
are wild nature today, its thick vegetation
surprising me as I look down the cliff

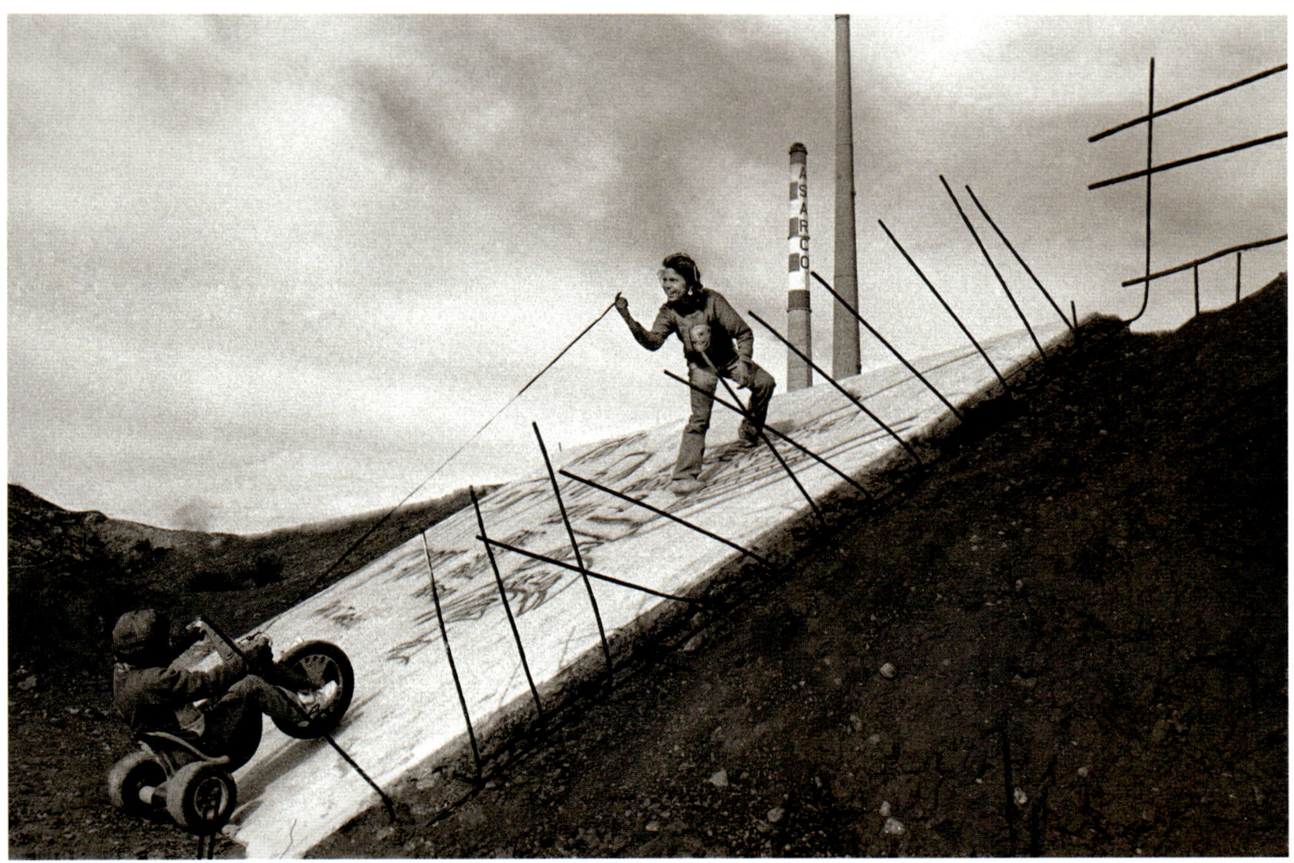

Kids on the levee. Juárez, Mexico, 1990.

where I fell, the sign on the boundary
warning me to show respect, new houses
destroying the mountain as the washed-
out arroyo of childhood is declared
to be protected ground.

Everything that Comes before Reason, Aguirre Springs, Organ Mountains

The deepest tree of ebony
emerges through the canyon

thousands of feet above
the desert floor.

Water runs into crevices,
the sun making the rattlesnake

end its music, a lone hawk
forming its own fire against

the sheer towers of time that
bow in their troubled light.

The piercing tree of ebony
brakes the sky in blue circles

that disappear into shifting
mountains, poetry of languages

colliding with shadows on
peaks as a pile of black rocks

is discovered in the middle
of the trail.

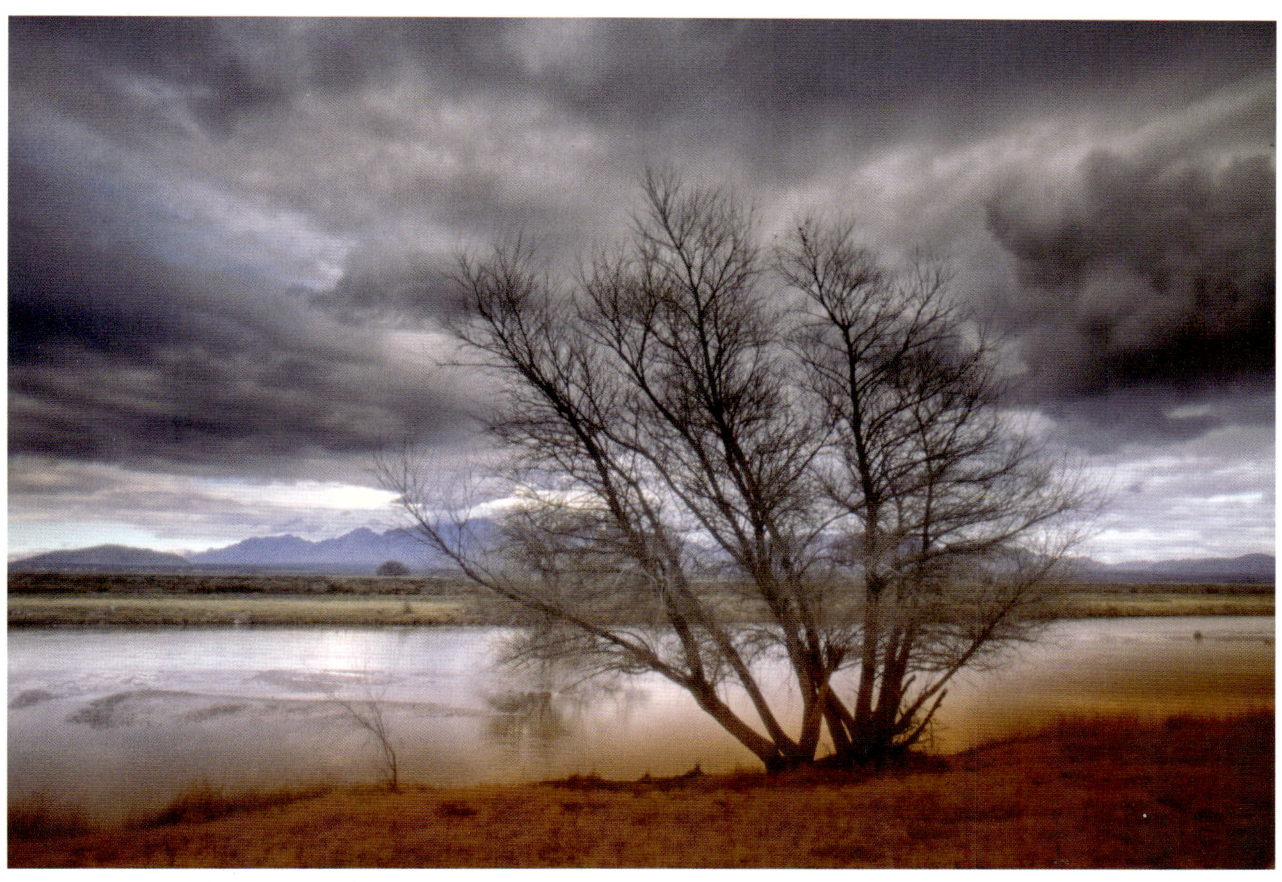

Lonely tree. Rio Grande, Southern New Mexico, 1989.

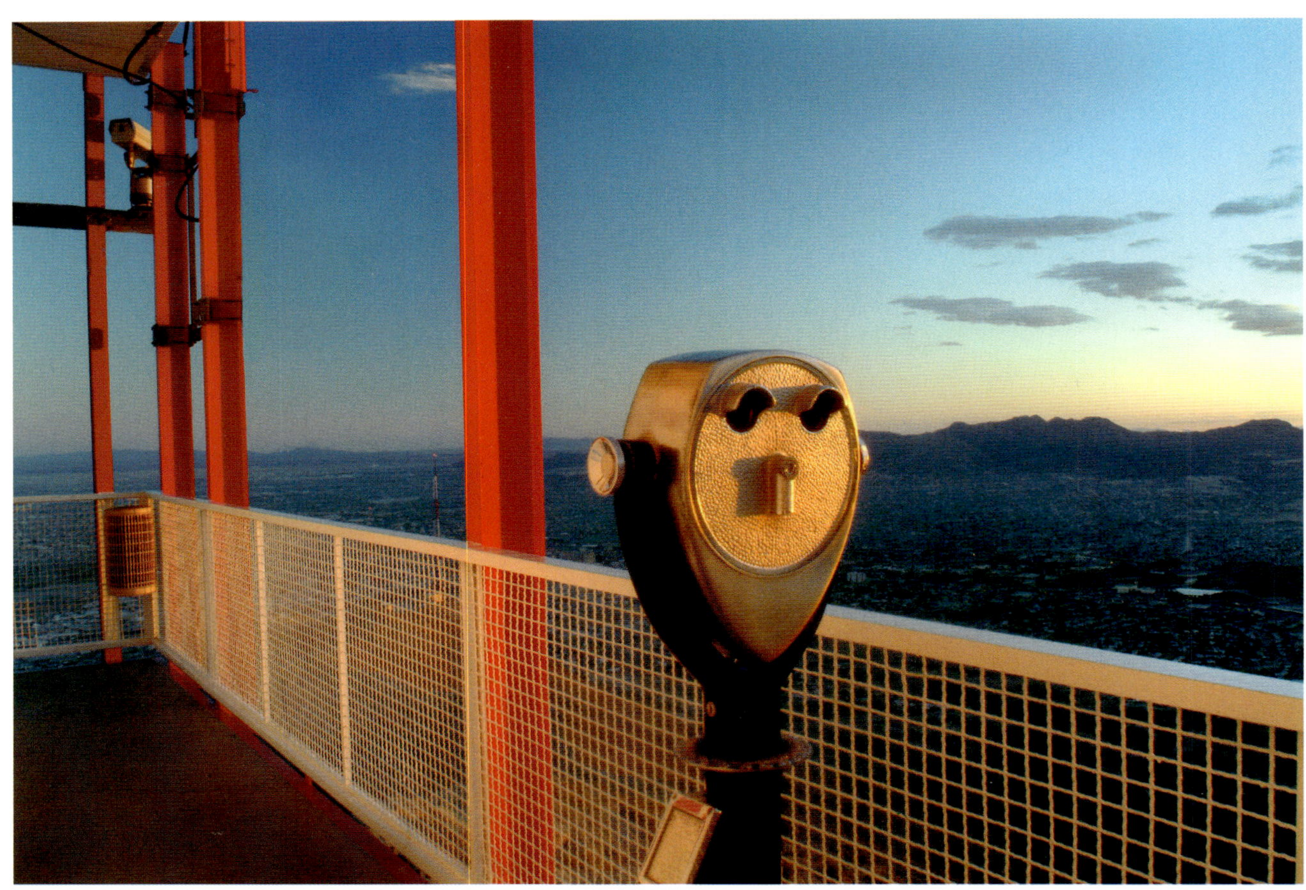

La Frontera overlook. El Paso, Texas, 2001.

Trying to Write Poetry

There is a village in the wilderness
of the desert stars.
When I look up, the heart traces
the light from one word to the next,
each thought collecting like dust on
the window that leads to the hidden
canyons, confined spaces where little
gods sit like mighty rocks glistening
in the troubled heat.

They trace the yucca fields with
fear that drops into flowers of sand,
the great kiss of wind and erosion
a mute hollow in the throat of
the wandering man leading him
to a cistern in the rocks where
water drips and moisture on my
lips keeps me mouthing what I say.

There is an arroyo, a cut in
the earth that waits for me to sing,
yet to sing would mean hiding further
into the cliffs, sharp arms of ocotillo
and prickly pear avoiding me
because they would end my song
and a fossil would rewrite my lyrics
in the sand.

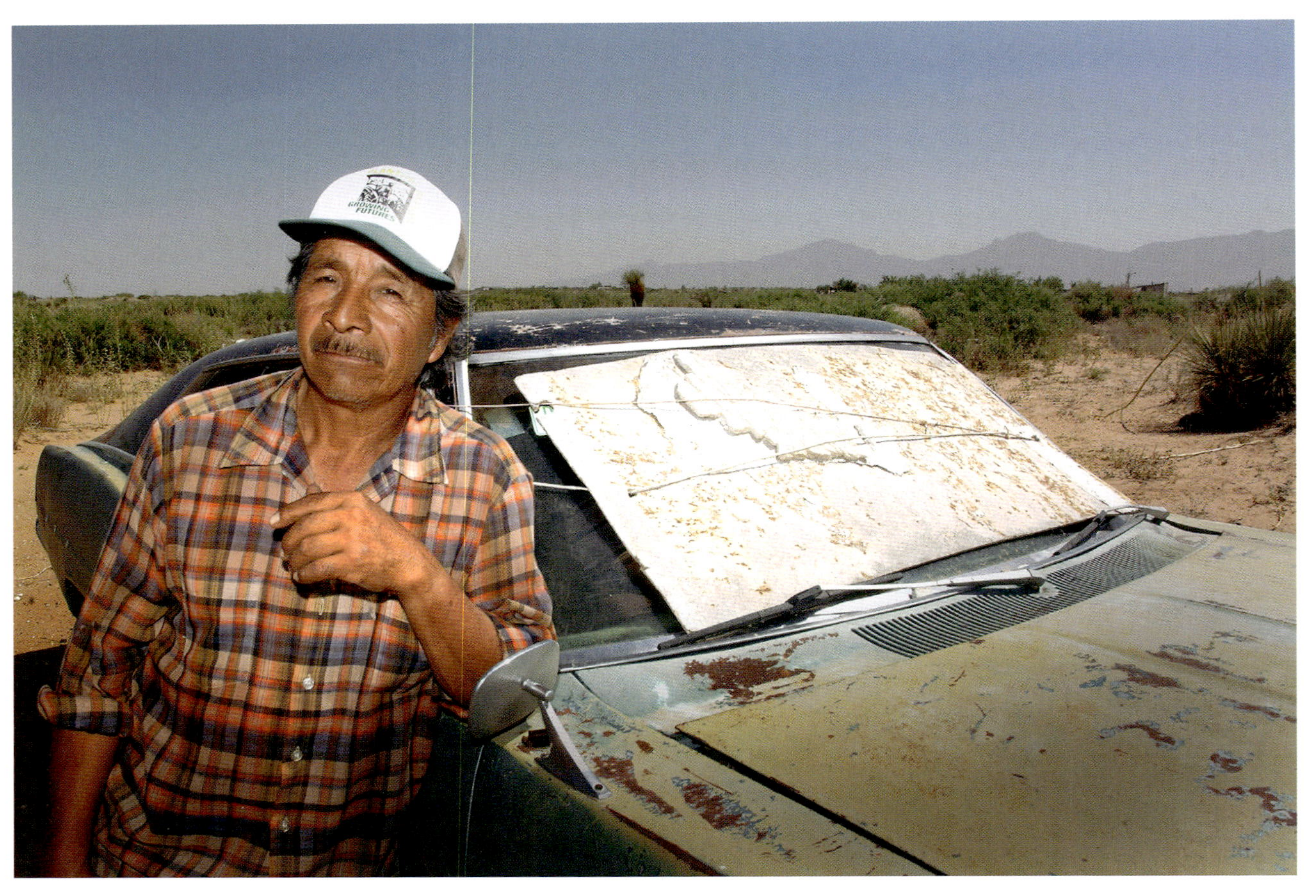

Martin. Lomás de Poleo, Juárez, Mexico, 2007.

Pray Lizard

He is motionless
like hair carved
on the rock.

Green tail,
sleek blue body
with a red bubble

that throats the world,
bloats for a second,
then disappears when

I kneel in the grass
to retrieve
my eyeglasses.

Looking for the Scorpion

Looking for the scorpion that sprang
under the leaves, I find a caterpillar
crawling over the mud, the yellow
scorpion darting into the ground
as if it were never there.

I grew up with scorpions everywhere—
on the walls, under the bed, in my shoes,
even on the ceiling where they dropped
onto clothes or the bed at night.

When they quit appearing one year,
I realized they had won by becoming
the mystical whips of yesterday,
their tails erect as if stinging the heart
was the natural way out.

Looking for the creature, I poke
the caterpillar, the hooked tail of
the scorpion parting the leaves
because sunlight is the chosen thing
that traces my startled face.

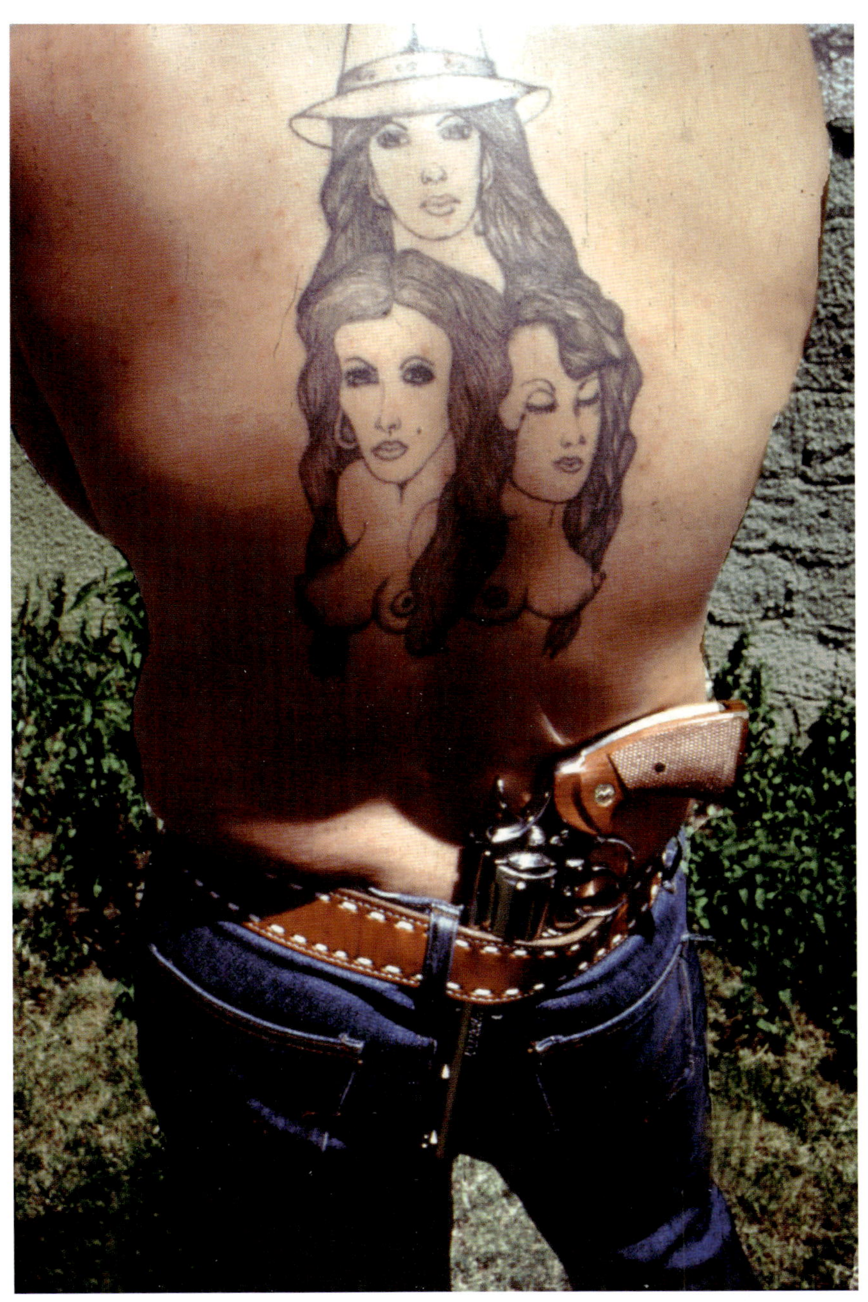

Federale with a gun. Juárez, Mexico, 1985.

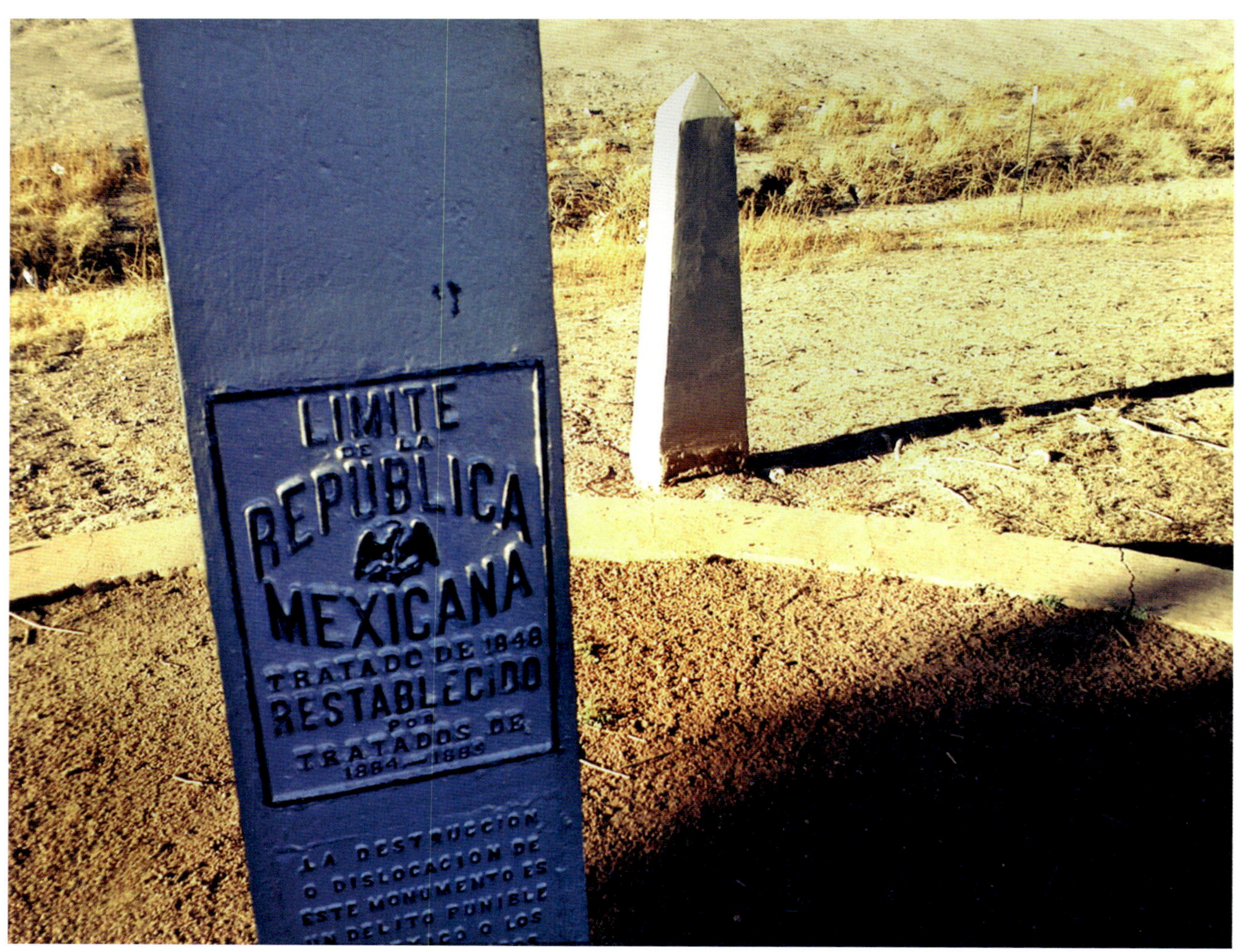

Border marker. Chamizal, El Paso, Texas, 2012.

Bilingual

Boy's voice reciting
in English and Spanish,

his voice echoing the suffering
over the caging of the family

at the border. He is forced
to speak in superstitious rhythm,

pronouncing words of love
mistaken for doubt, sounds

of courage untranslatable.
Young voice writes stanzas

without knowing what they
mean since no one admits

these things must be said
in only one tongue.

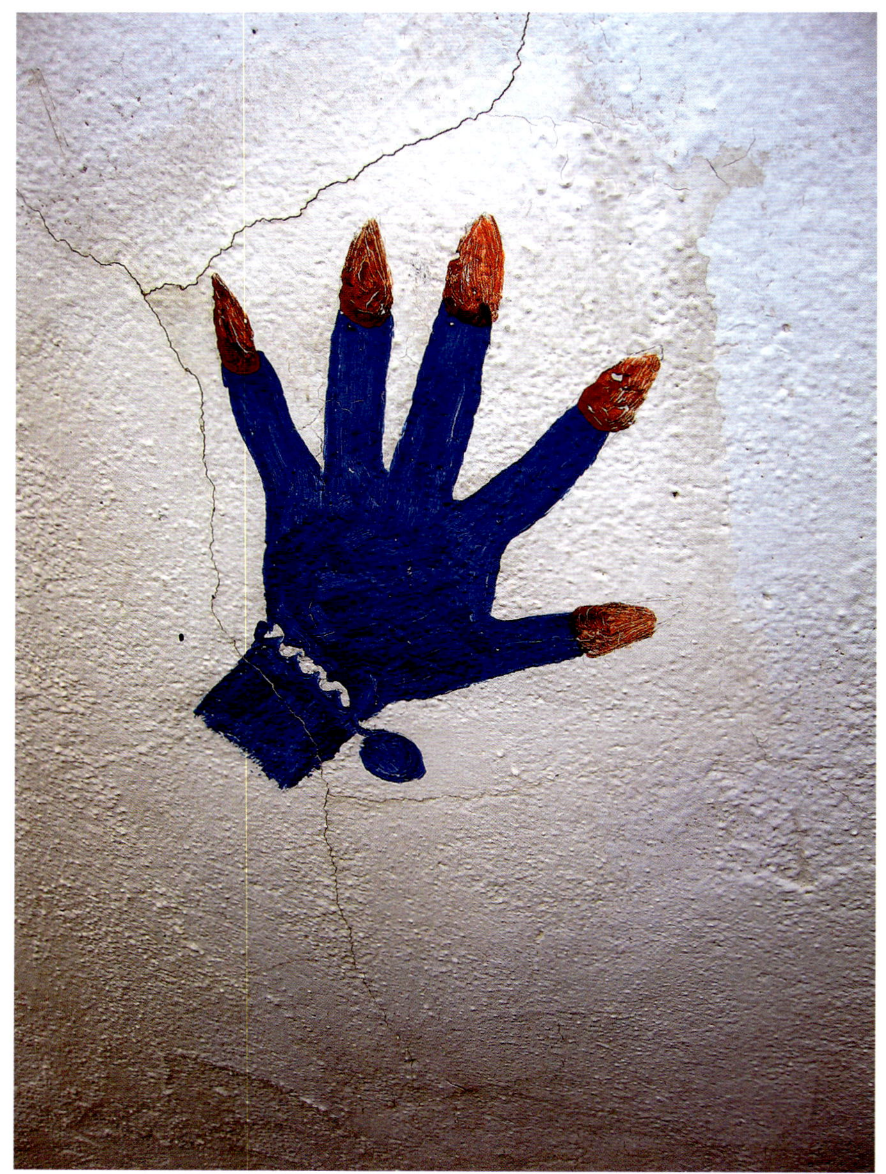

Crazy hand. El Paso, Texas, 2005.

The Cave at Bear Paws Site, Franklin Mountains

No one has come out of it in years,
ancient pictograph of bear paws guarding
the opening high on the rocky slope
where the sun brands the rocks
and blinds the host.

The cave is narrow and dark,
its pictures deformed by a few
human hands, though rockslides
have taken care of that, the drawing

of bear paws fading over time,
suburbs spreading nearby, colors
revealing a hole where the tongue
moans over cold stone.

Archaeologists dig, renaming
the earth to bring back the hour
of the bear when those who
disappeared within were
found on the other side.

No one has entered in years,
though the voice that stays is
the voice that rings inside, where
the bear paws are the flash
that opens the defiant heart.

Searching for Max Ernst in Sedona, Arizona

Search for the painter in the red cliffs,
his ceremony in the ancient footholds
on the walls where Ernst lived for years,
slowing you down when the lechuga wraps
its thorny branches around your ankle,
pulling you into the river where invisible
cities have thrived for centuries.

Look under the rocks where the hands
of Christ are buried. Kick the saguaro
and study the worms in the roots, aroma
of seizura overcoming you in the well
where the totem seer drowned.

Give up the rattle from the snake you killed.
Pull it off your neck and stick it in your ear.
When the earthquake settles, open your eyes
in the canyon where the little stray dog ran
and never came out. Push Ernst's collection

of kachinas over the edge, the deity dolls
pulling your arms into his painting of a man
and woman on fire, their legs twisted in
the arms of their dying mothers.
When the kachinas hit the bottom, blue dust
they stir will show you where the artist took
off his mask he could never paint.

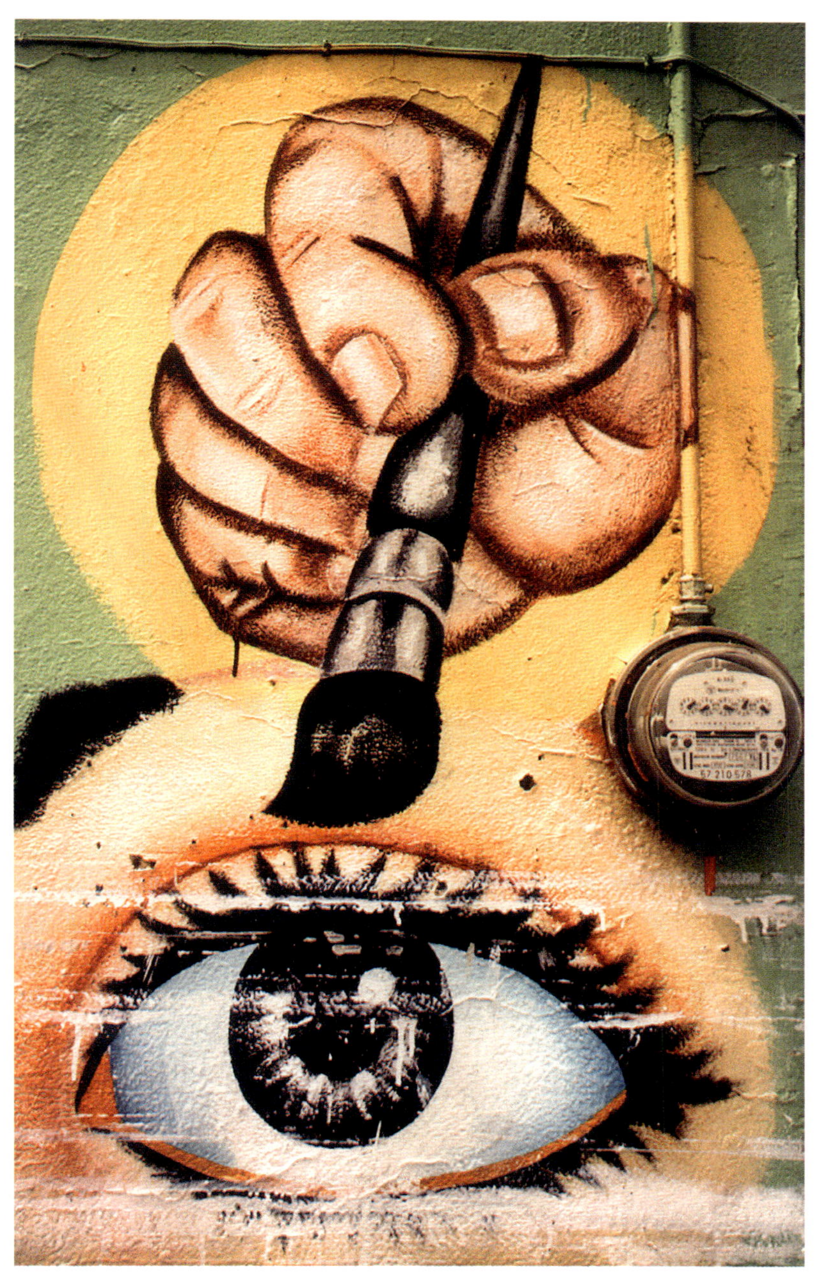

The Eye of Juárez. Juárez, Mexico, 1984.

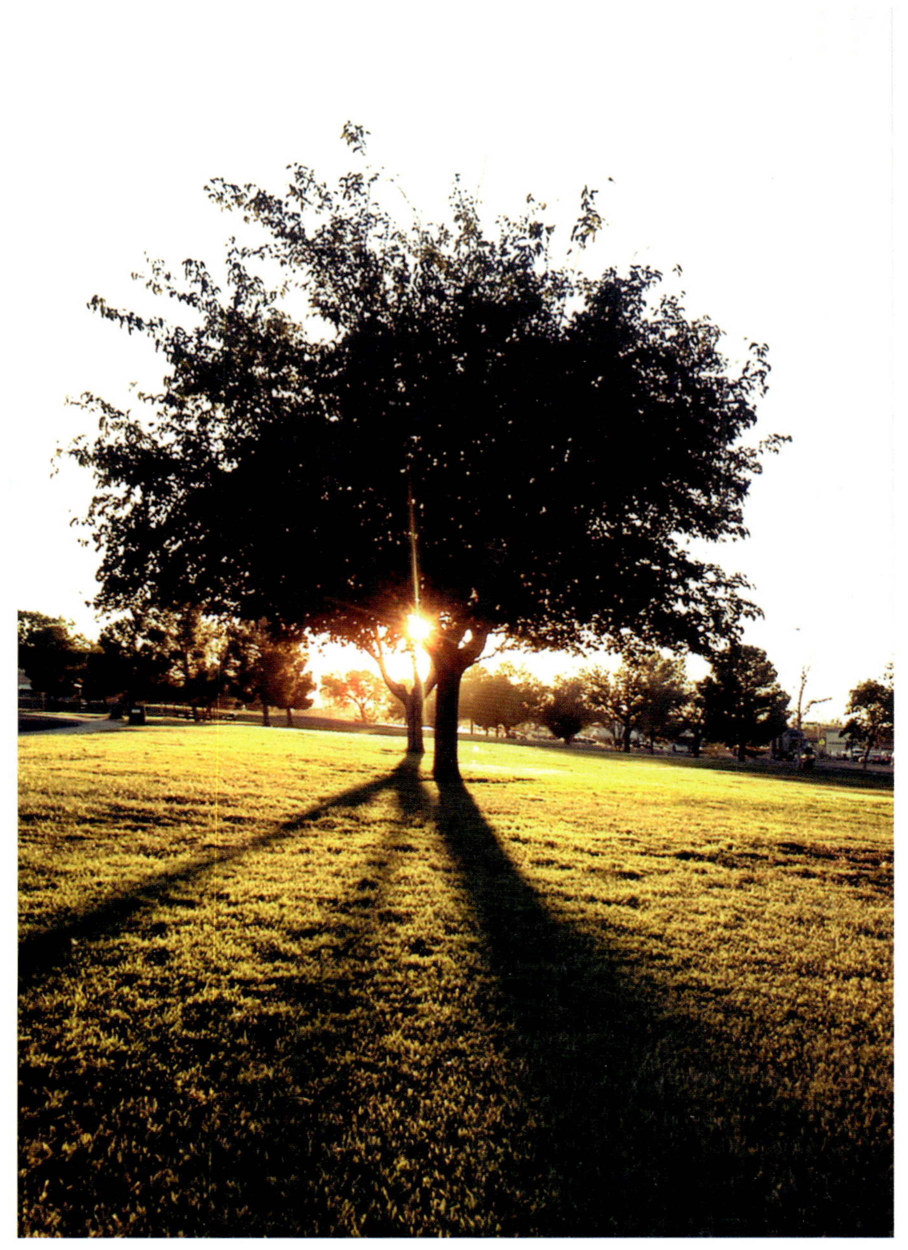

Chamizal summer. El Paso, Texas, 2012.

Memorize the Trees

Cottonwoods and salt cedars
growing along the river where
I wanted to plant my own trees
where none had grown, branches
and green shapes erasing what
I demanded to see.

I stood on the bank as the rising
water took the trees beyond
the curve in the river where
I dared myself to swim across.
I never did and lost more trees.

Once, I grabbed a low branch
before letting go over the blue plane,
leaves flaking in my hands to make
sure I would never forget this
crumbling that takes place each time
the level of the river goes down.

I am too far away now to reshape
the trees in a light containing
what I want you to believe—
I never left those trees, but let
the season of hungry rain soak
the water as they surrounded
my first thoughts and left me
muddy and waiting at the gate.

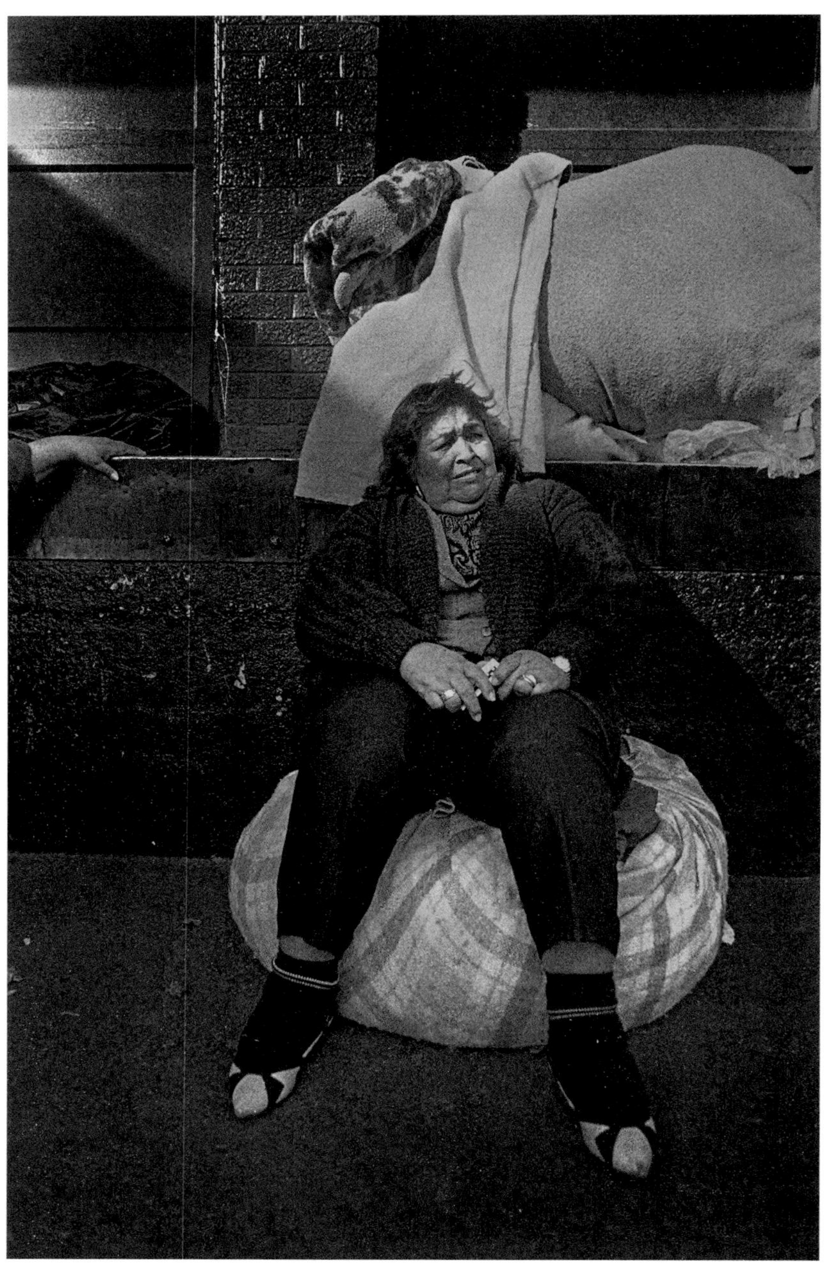

Queen of the ropas. El Paso, Texas, 1995.

Solitude

Solitude searches for hands
to paint what can't be revealed.

It is the river going dry, leaving
torn shoes and shirts behind.

Solitude is a candle melting
inside a clay bowl,

the river returning to flow
in arms of vibrant mud.

Solitude is encircling my desert
town instead of burying it.

It is the cottonwood shedding
a third eye from its bark.

Mesilla Moon

He opened the arched doorway
and found the moon wanting its exit,

stepped into the ancient courtyard where
the two-headed lizard once roamed the wall.

The last time he saw it, the moon was full and
the creature guarded the gate to the other side.

He walked like a boy and dreamed of the moon
like a man being served mescal in a dying cup.

When the moon over Mesilla moved behind
the clouds, his Mexican angel stood under

an enormous cottonwood and shook.
It was a poem and a greeting, a rhythm of

knowing what took place under the sky,
how the moon guided him to a blessing inside.

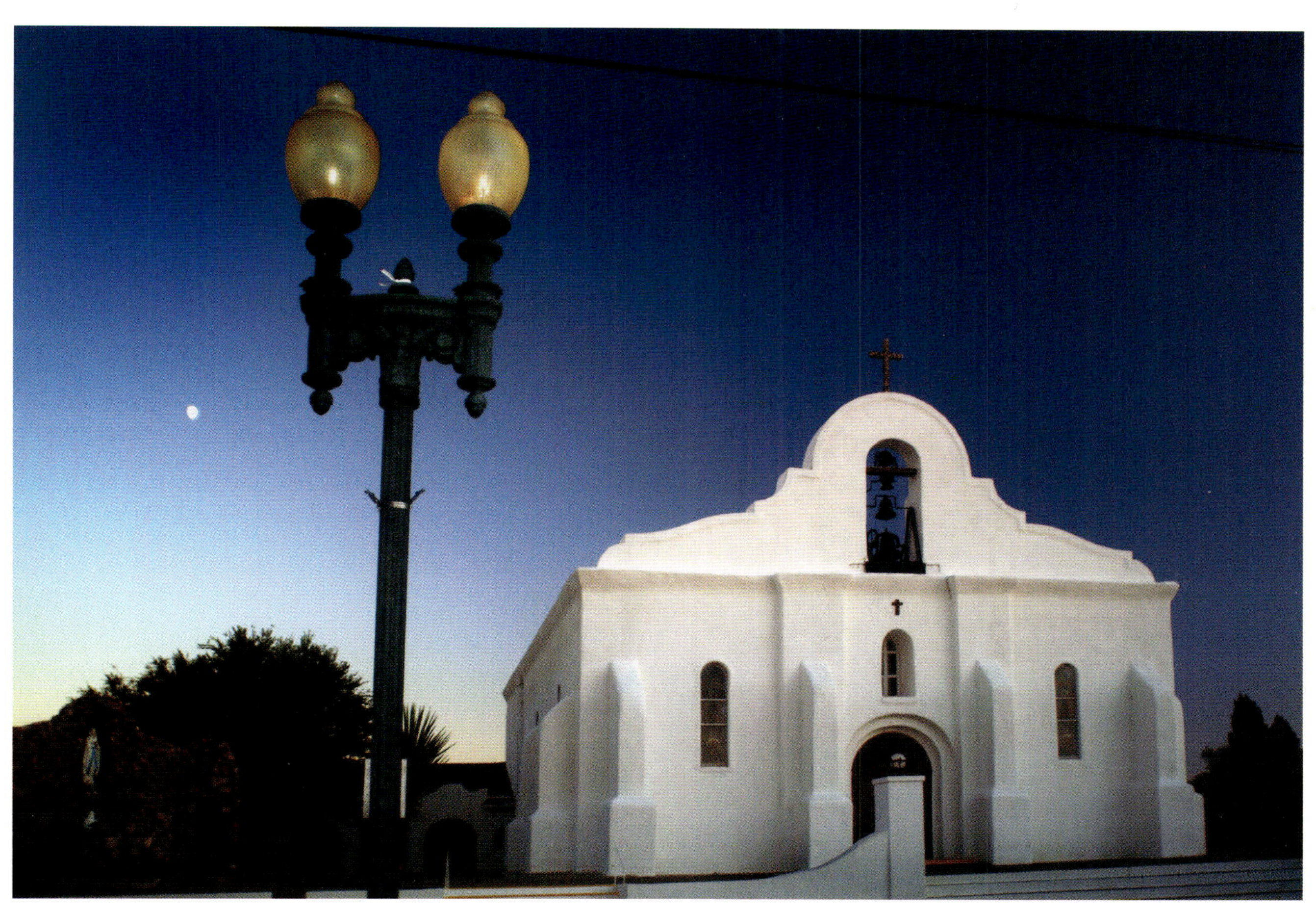

Presidio Chapel. San Elizario, Texas, 2003.

The Border Is a Line

The Mexican border is a line between
faith and the shackled dream.

When people cross it, the highways
lead north and west.

When they are stopped and taken,
the green vans go south.

The border is a line between
imagination and the truth—

those who make it will not return,
the line leading to bodies in lost graves.

The line extends from birth to death,
though the mountains get in the way,

the line curving around them
to gather strength.

The line becomes a long sentence
when the labor matters, survivors

straightening the line to align it
with the relentless sun, stars falling

above the hole where they hide.
Even the bloodline from a plastic

bottle of water to a picture of La Virgen
de Guadalupe is sacrificed at the wire

because the Mexican border is a line
between faith and its sharpest point—

a line that is infinite, unstoppable,
and keeps coming this way.

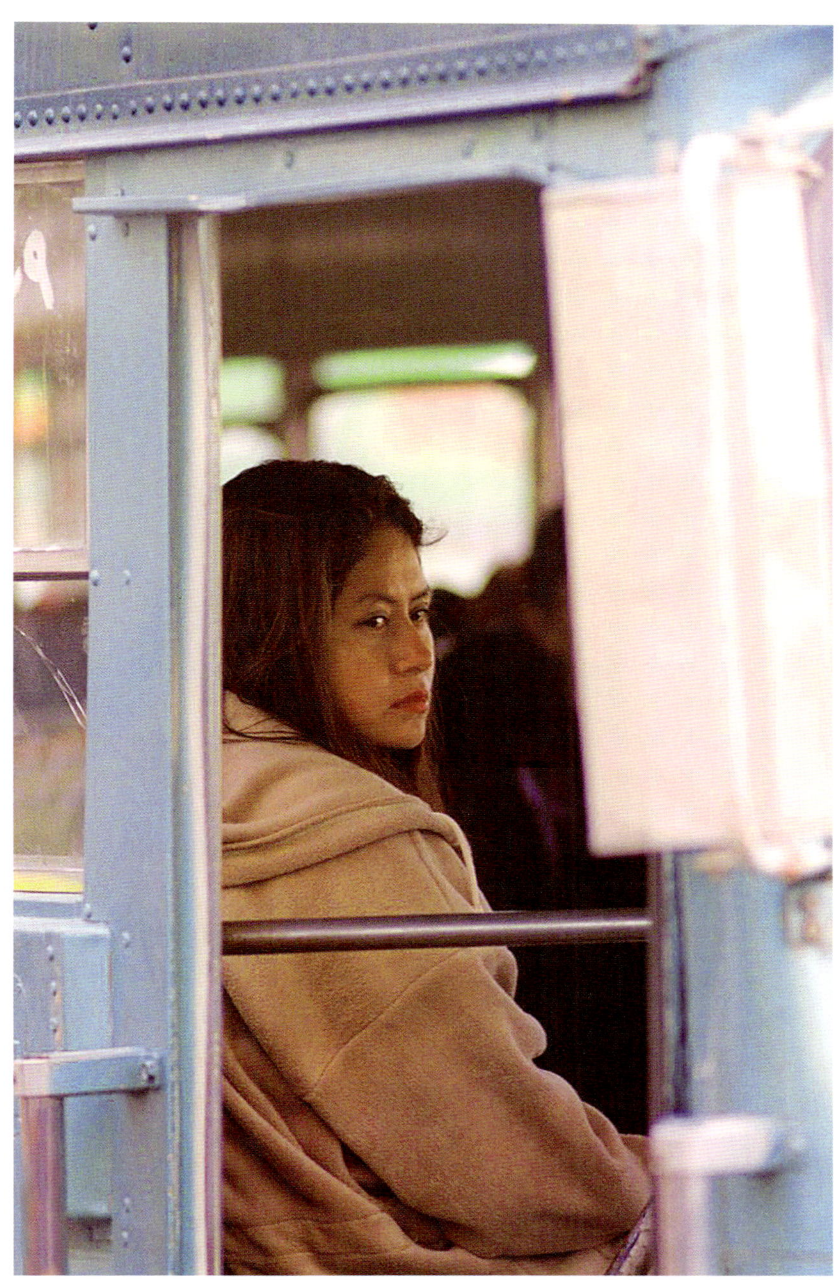

Girl on a bus. Juárez, Mexico, 2004.

BRUCE BERMAN AND LAWRENCE WELSH

Dyer's Angels

how enlivened
by neon
or the stagecoach
towards oro grande:
now
a miner's shack
to know
or get
their wings
they become
anonymous
like desert bones
and then
forget to
remember
a way
away
or down
this line

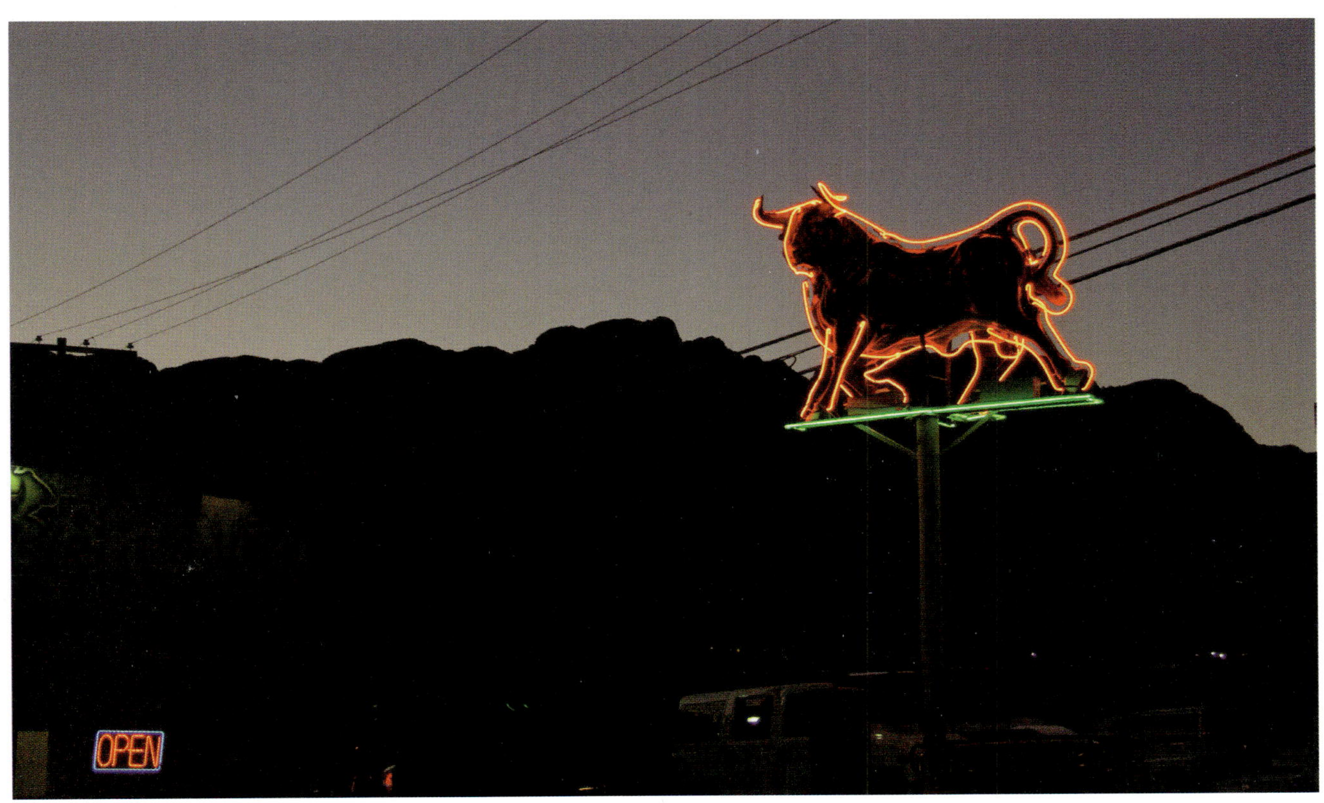

Neon bull. El Paso, Texas, 2012.

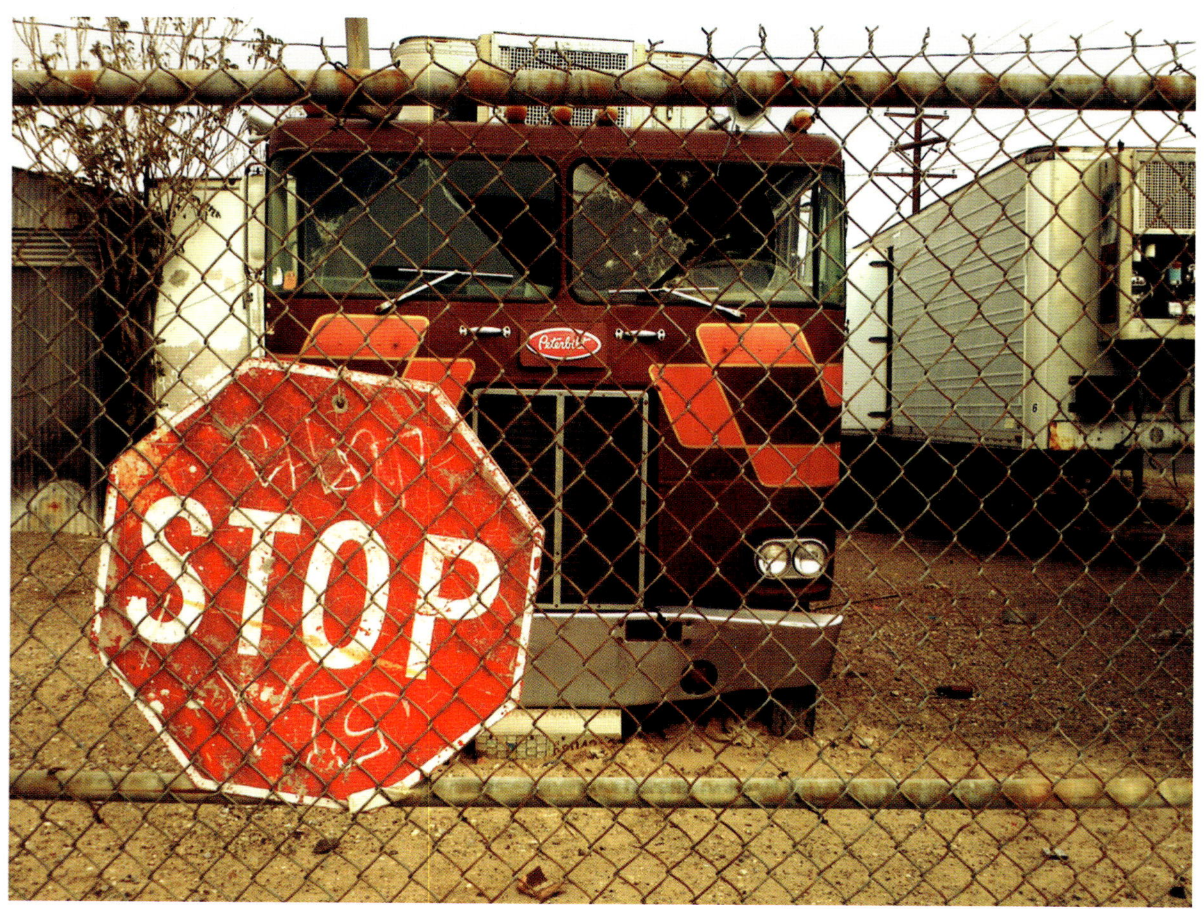

Stopped. El Paso, Texas, 2012.

The Crossing

miles and miles
of chain link
doubling up
tripling up.
we're crashing through
slashing through
silver and blue
train tracks:
the huffing and puffing
the racing speed
passing into
zones of
stability
instability
to new opportunities
chased
in the searchlight
beam

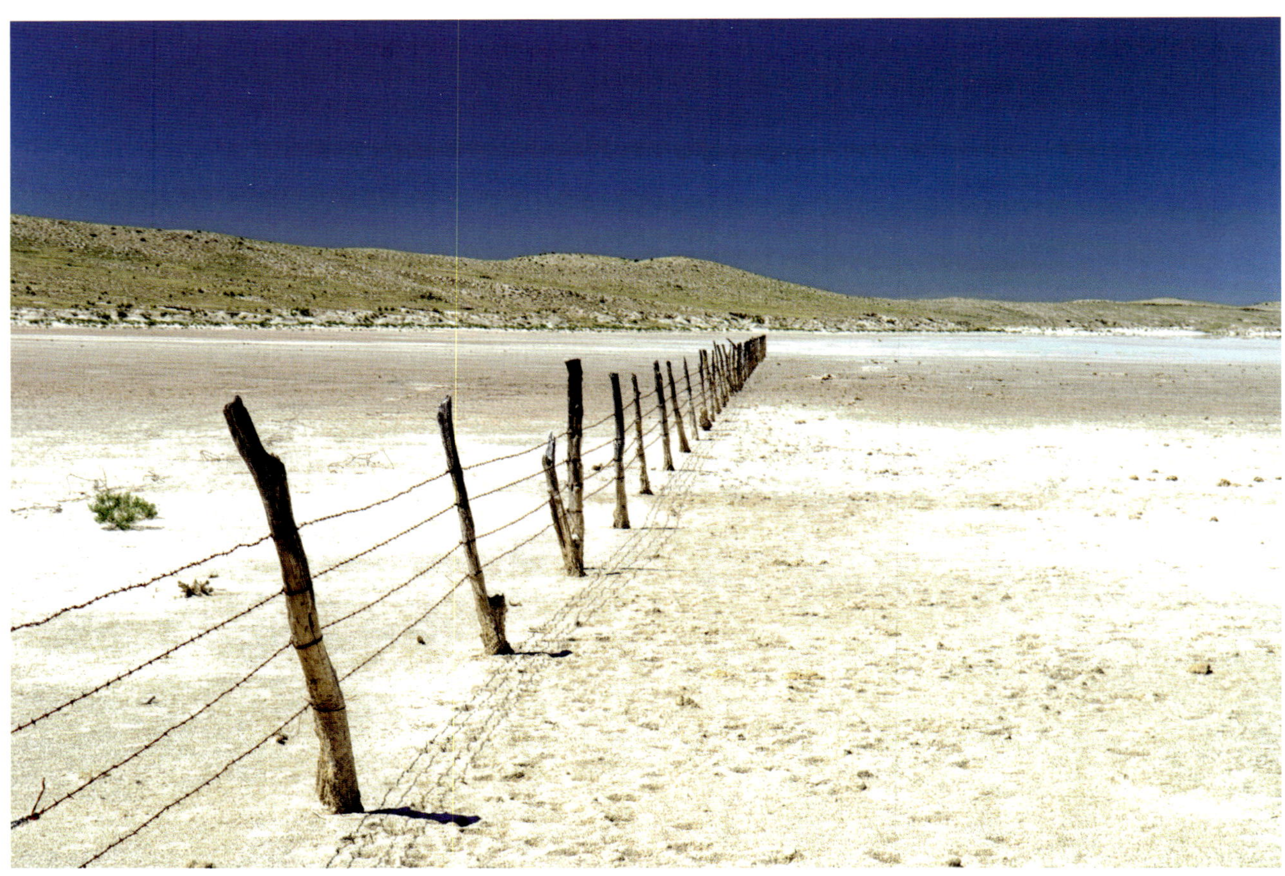

Badlands fence. New Mexico, 2010.

Desert Moon Driver

it's barbed wire
around the river too
around the bend
to sunland
where cristo rey
is no spotlight
but alabaster
under the
white moon
as enough
reflection
illumination
to keep them
moving on

Virgin / San Lorenzo

into glass
the pink hues
are blue too
with roses and lilies
they all become
resurrected
in place
as a giver
of tasks believes
after sunset
a fading too
into the momentary
darkness
the midnight lights
only
stars outside

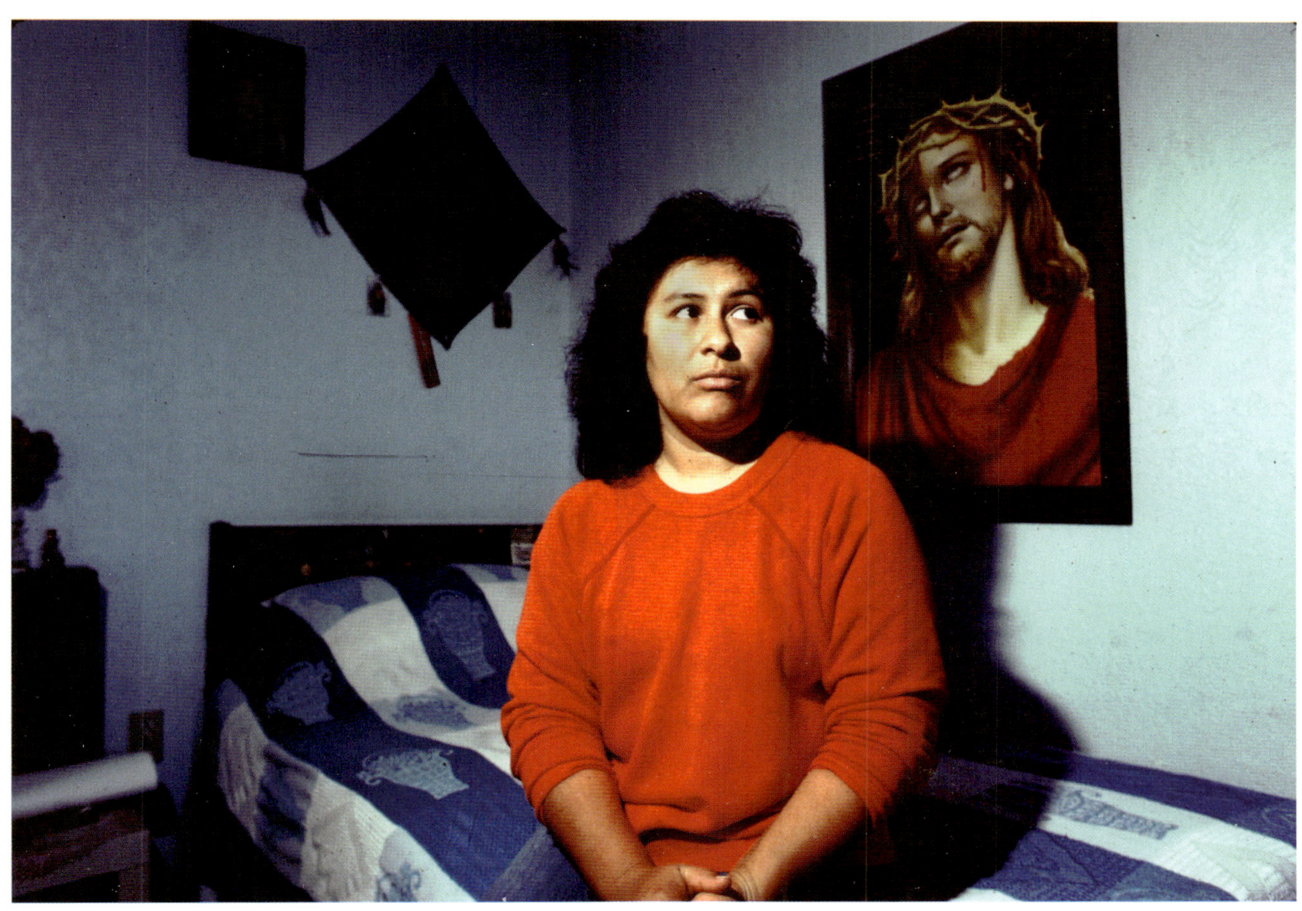

Jesus y Maria. Texas, 1989.

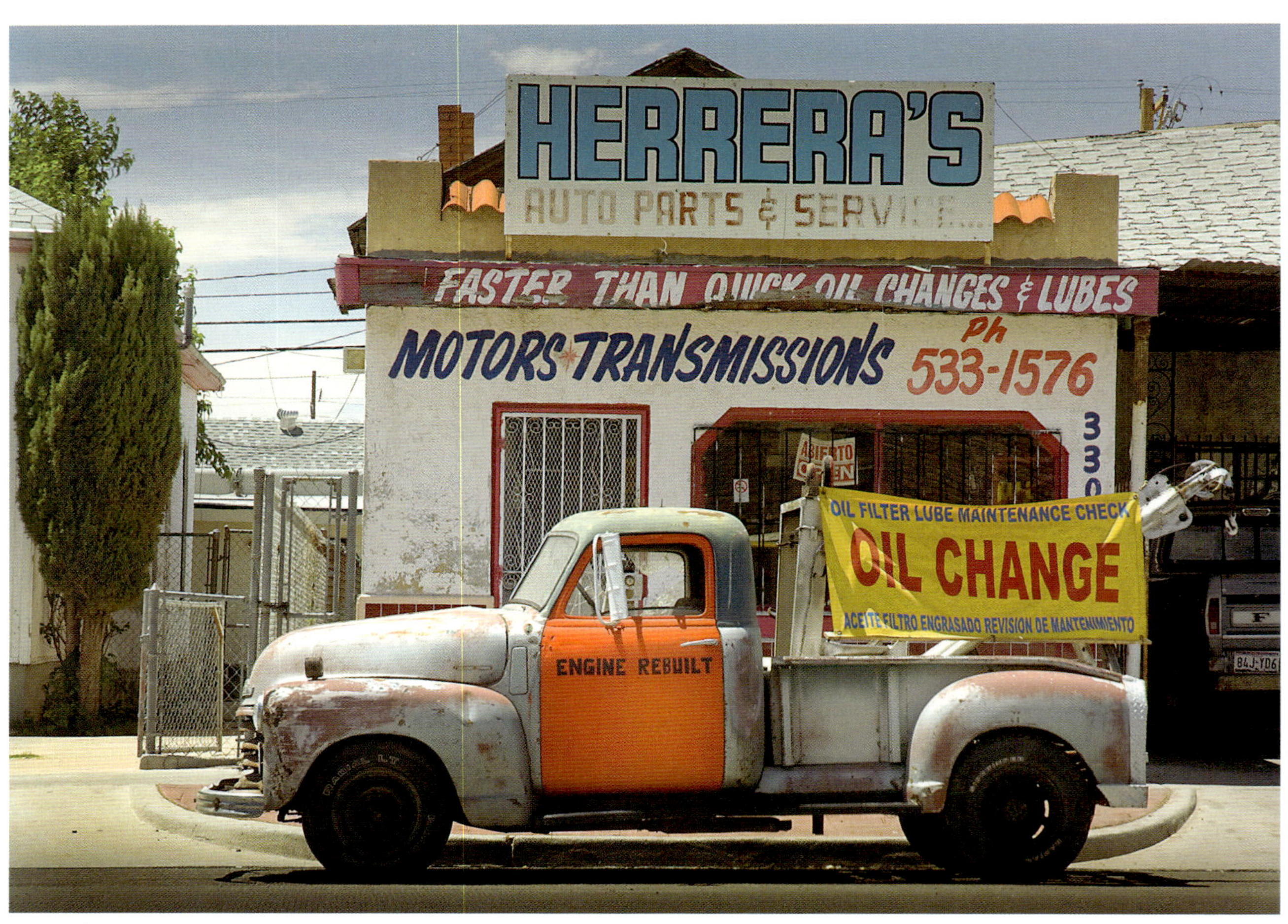

Herrera's truck. El Paso, Texas, 2010.

Road to El Paso—Revisited

essence
might blind
the doniphan push
to canutillo

so let it die
to forget
what i came
here for

a burning
a stripping down
the casting off
of masks
of invincibility
and then
only
the road in

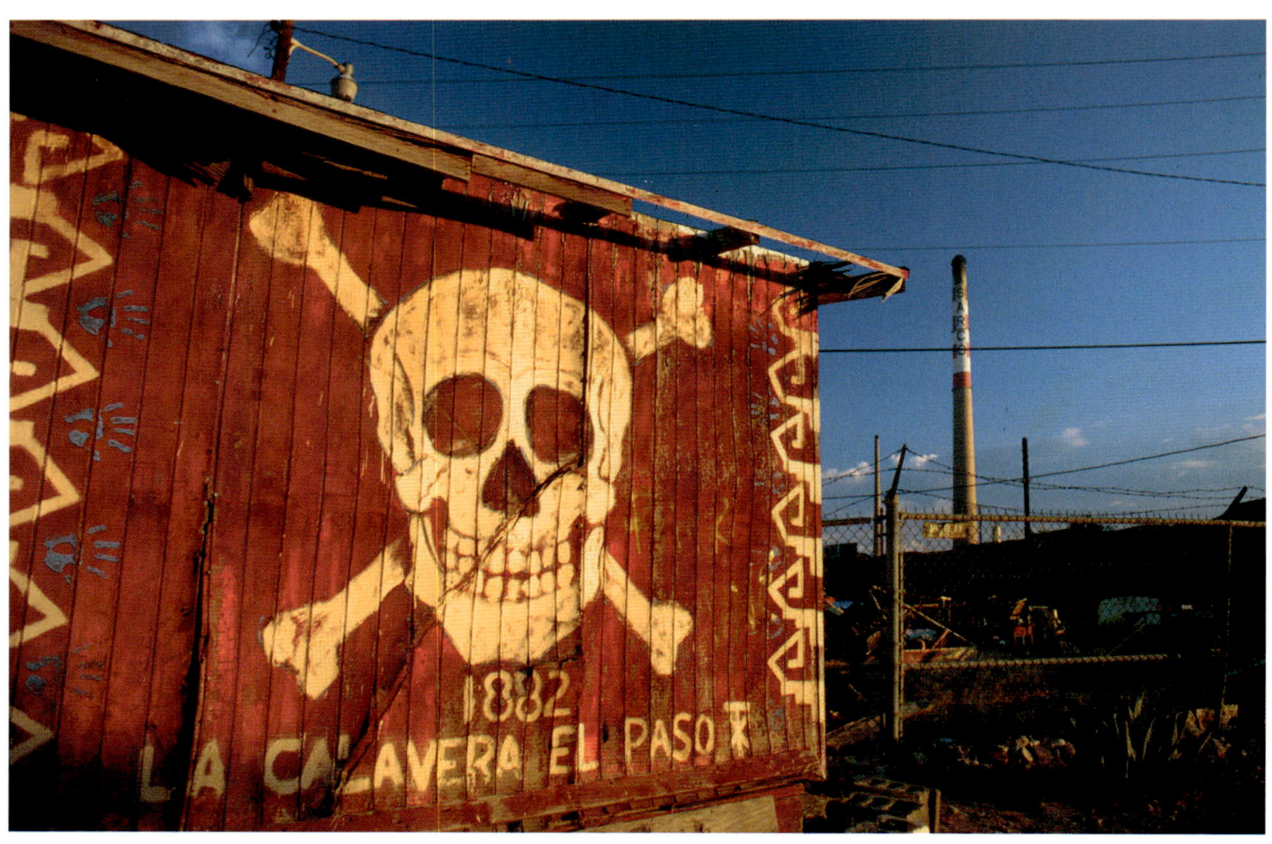

La Calavera de ASARCO. El Paso, Texas, 1984.

May 31

in things
the window says
anapra chaser
mimosa blossom
asarco skeleton
and la calavera's pitch
for smeltertown graves
where villa and madero
became
the way we walk
our thoughts and deceits
w/ cannon smoke
zigzag smoke
caught in mesquite
and medicine trees

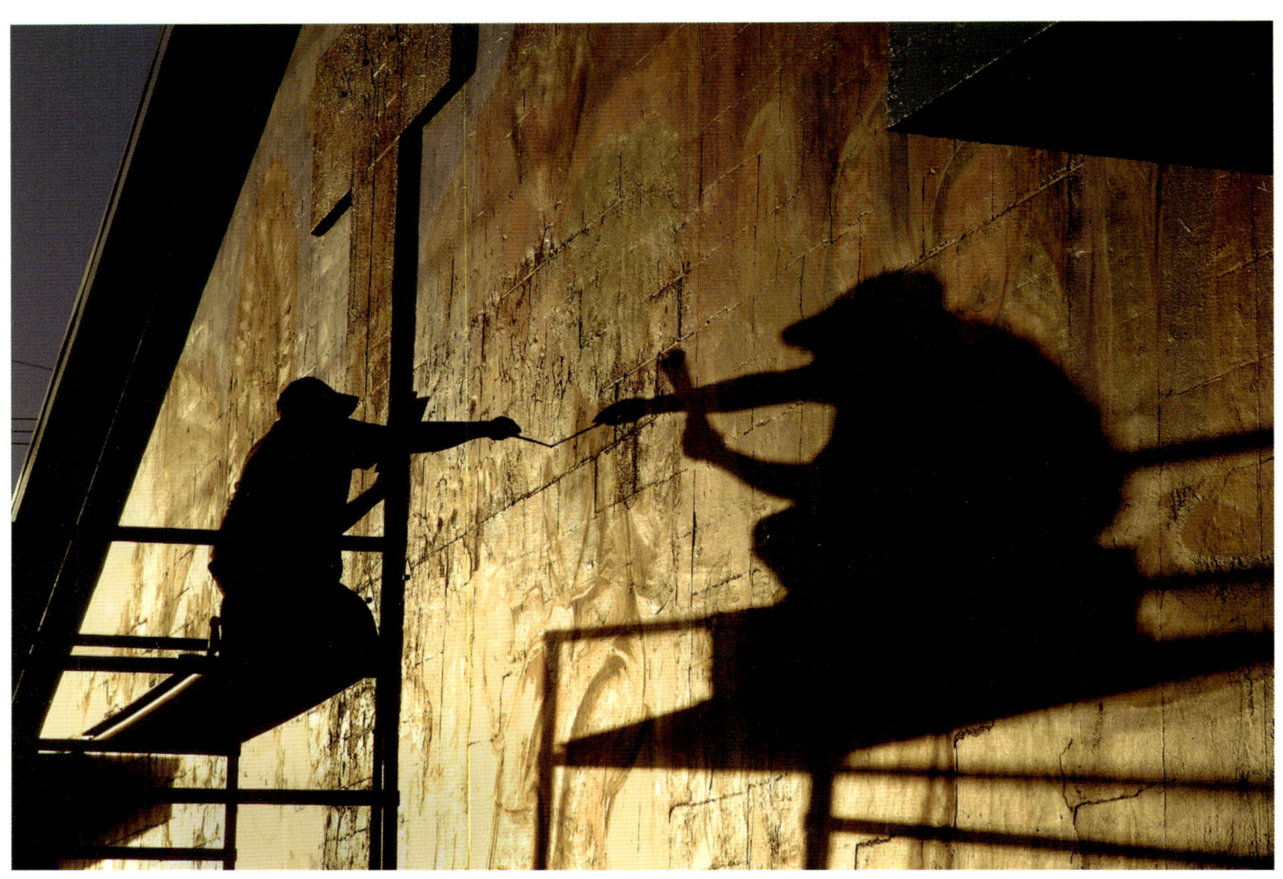

Muralista. Segundo Barrio, El Paso, Texas, 2006.

Shadow Burn

gold
on sunland
at cemex
covers where
the rio grande
goes
or
west texas sun
owns
southern
new mexico
and throws
what's left
on the mountain
and disappears on
a local's wall

Mesa Blues

a simplicity for eyes
for nothing's left to hold
only sun and dust
and a promise to reach
cristo rey backwards
like now forgetting
the crucifixion
sometimes for the dreamer—
boys and girls waiting
to start over here
and make a track
the pumas and coyotes
will only see

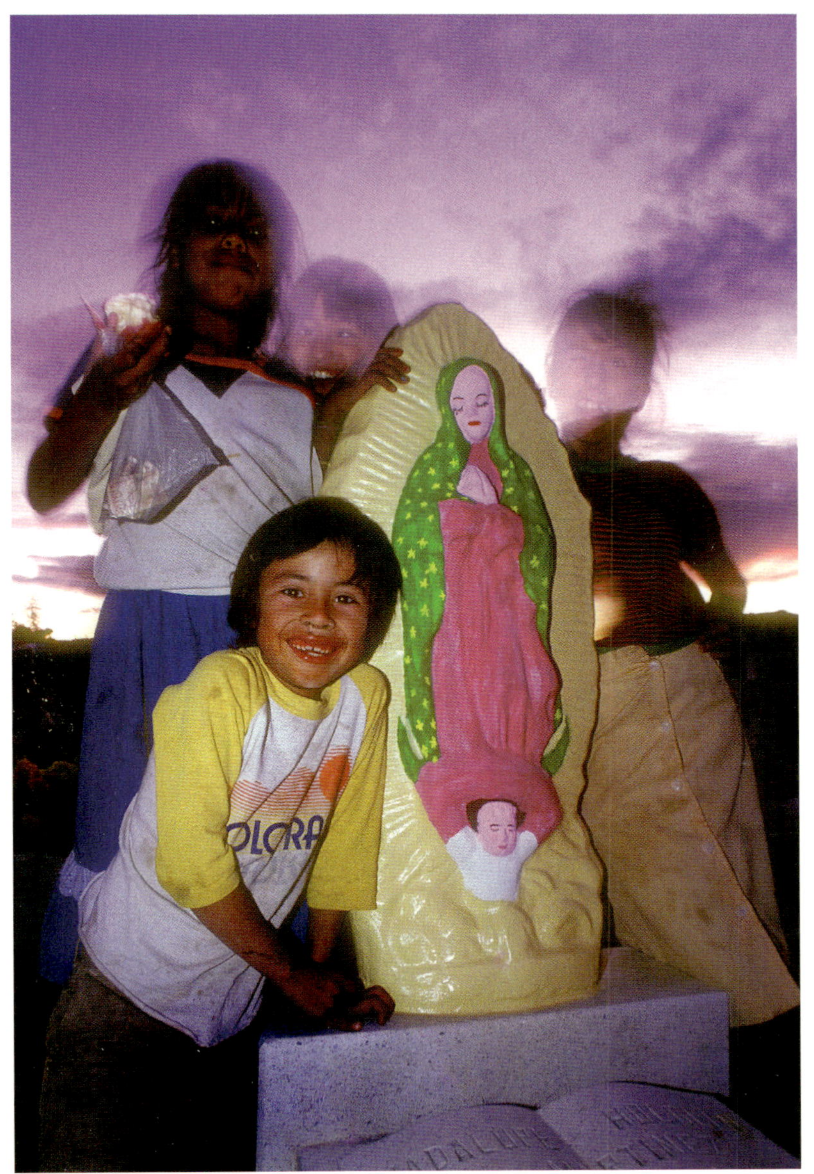

El Panteón de Juárez. Juárez, Mexico, 1984.

Smeltertown Crucifix

hidden by the river
in creosote, chamisa
the border patrol never sees
or the federal boundary authority
with binoculars
for chihuahua's best slip across
like swimmers, crawlers
for the sides
or down on sand
i see a mirage
or shadows kneeling
their eyes and hands
pointing only
to the sun

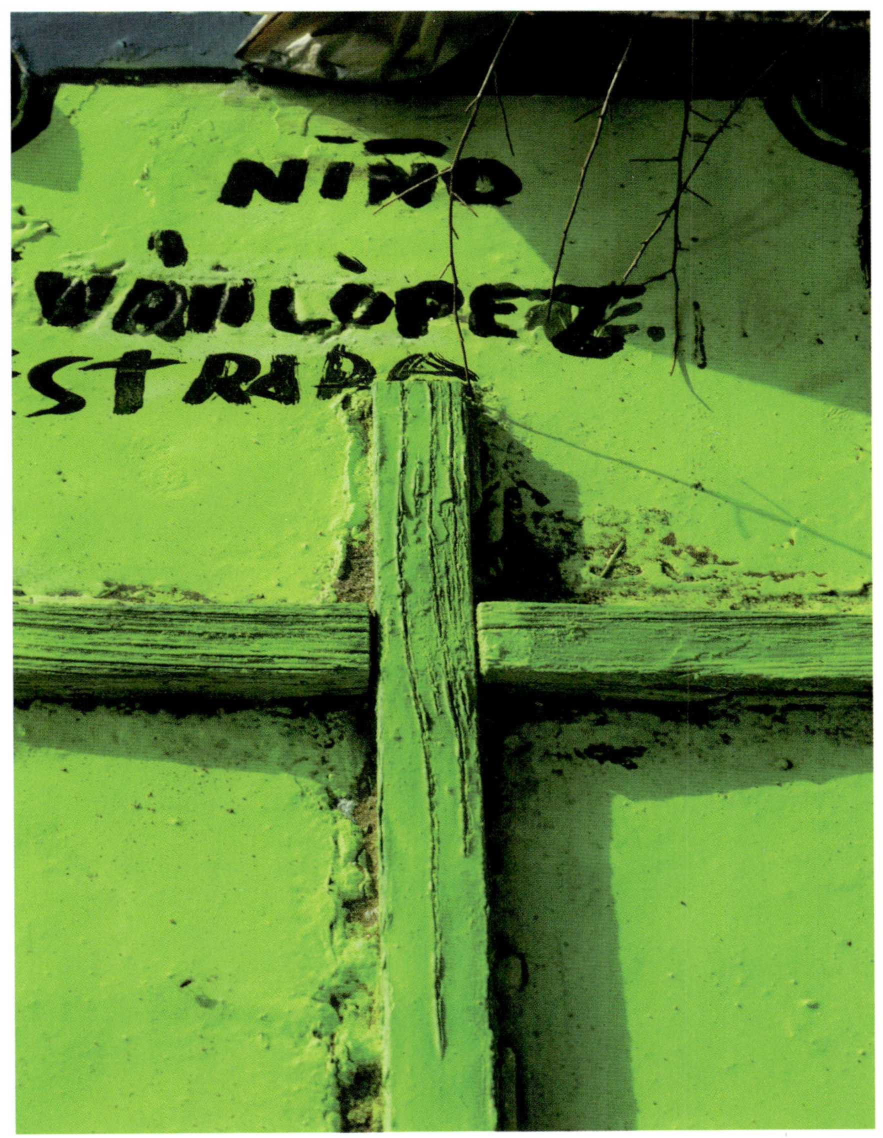

Niño. El Paso, Texas, 1989.

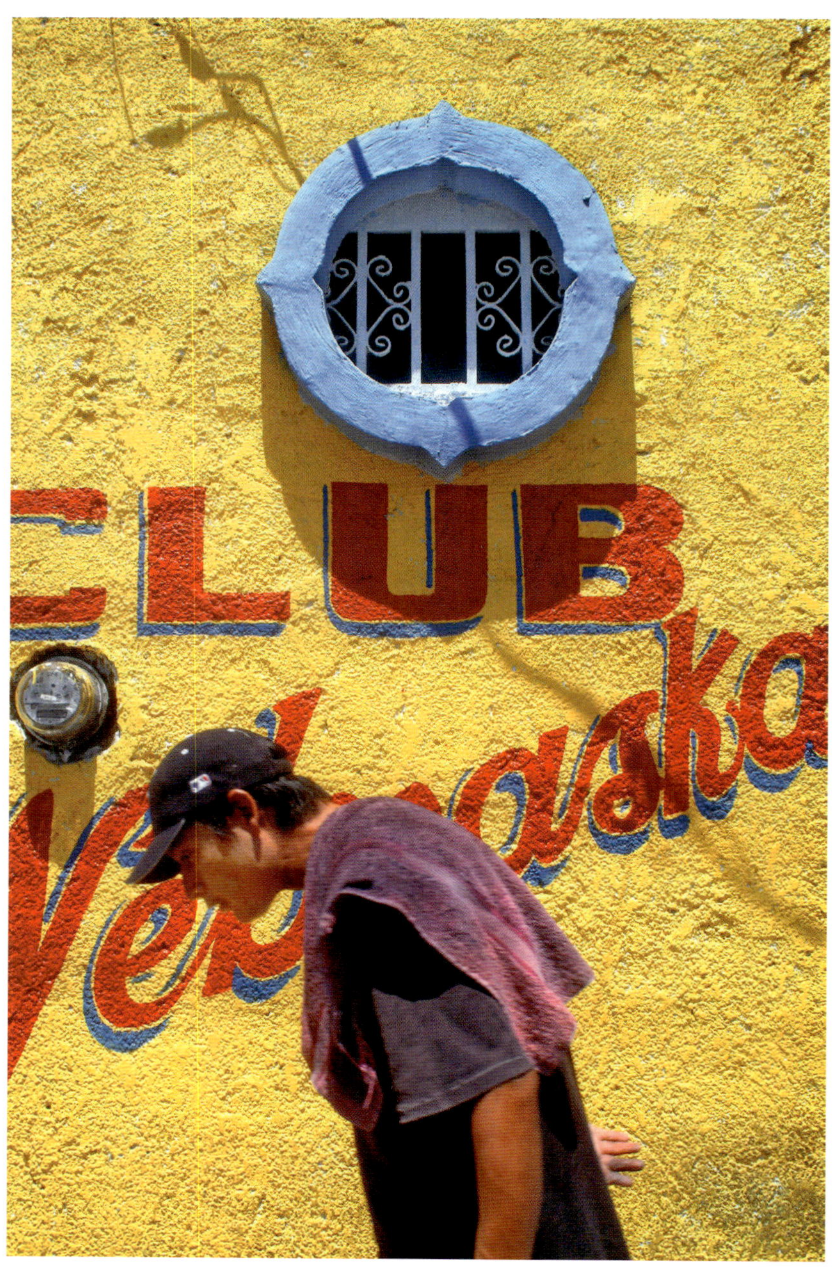

Ducking the photographer. Juárez, Mexico, 2004.

Last Exit: Doniphan

let cano's saloon supplant rosa's cantina
and remember buena vista still sees
anapra's line and the asarco stacks

let the rio grande / burlington northern
cut off for sale, for lease, for free
for underpass dreams are sunland park trotters
who make a pilgrimage to cristo rey

who dies dies here knows more
than smeltertown's resurrection
its orange eyes, black slag
and the souls who believed

give us permanence then for wanting this stretch
for it sees and grieves and helps us off our knees

that's good enough
for summer's coming on
and the heat already
as escapism
in mesquite trees

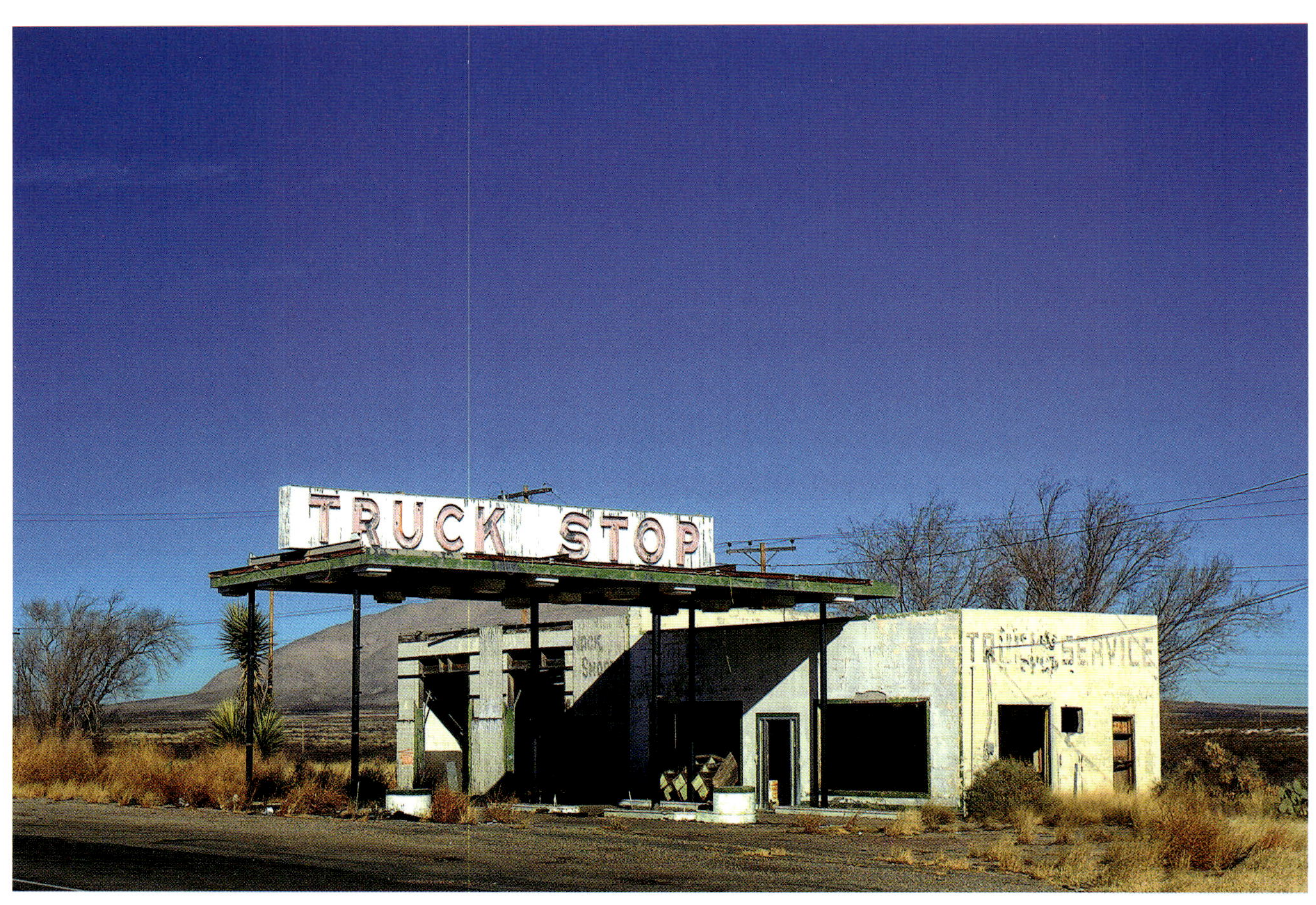

Abandoned truck stop. Sierra Blanca, Texas, 2009.

Socorro General Store

give vacancy
or beyond that:

boarded up
w/ cottonwood
in 1959

and now
no trespassing
the nothing for sale
not even
old pueblo road
or two hundred dreams
from la purisma

some say "gas"
in san elizario
or clint
good enough
as "trip"
just three
miles away

Toward Chinati

burnt
mountain
called
yellowed leaves
and coyotes
toward
javilina's path
turns out
around
soaks in
hot
mineral springs
stays at
el patron
and remains
out
of the shadows

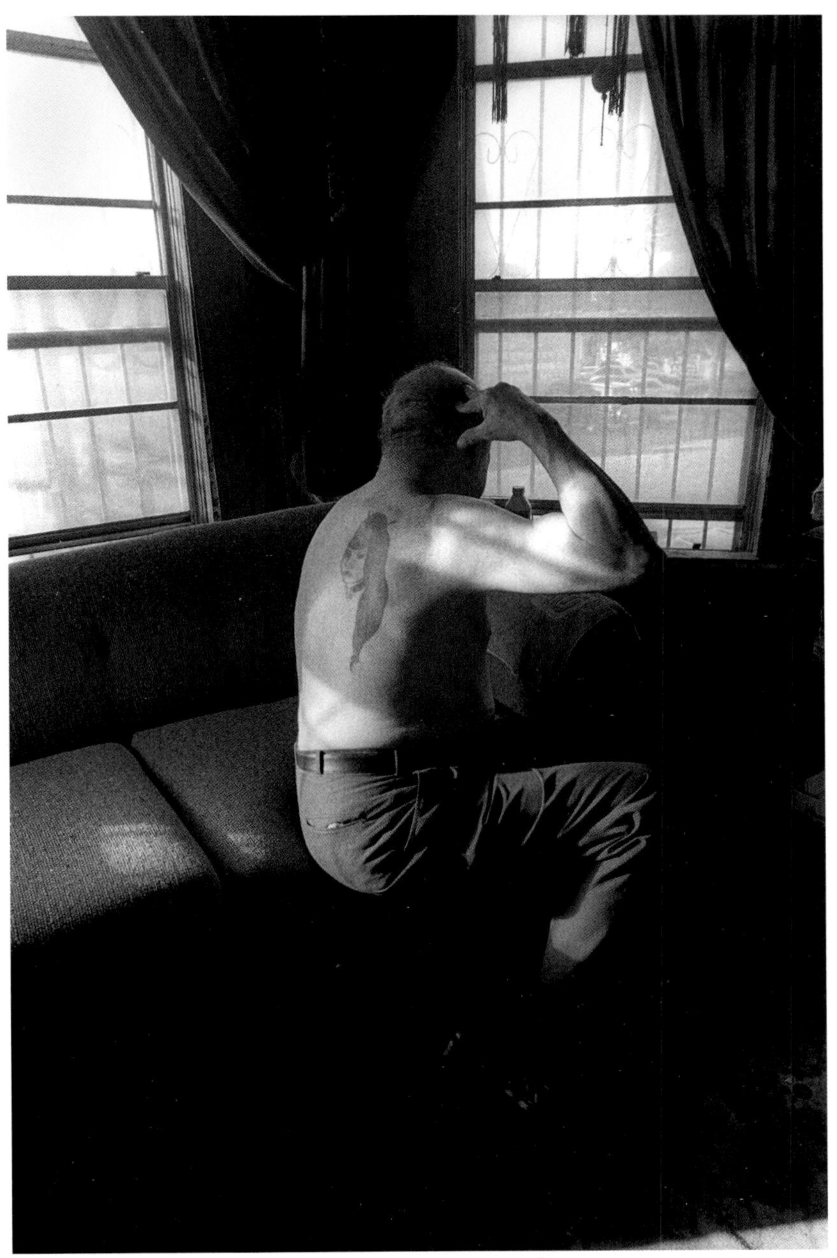

Chaplin before his date. The day Old Blue Eyes died, May 14, 1998.

Old Railroaders

and what they talk about
on canes
are old times of steel and oil
and coal fuel to fire the stove

i see coffee stains
on a santa fe caboose floor
retired in 1980

my son climbs the conductor's ladder
sits in his seat: ghosts on the tracks
the blood of american dreams
and waste won to win memories now:

everywhere they went
everywhere they've seen—

everywhere and back
and here again

for they remain
will remain
long after they're gone
into the dreams
of boys and men yet
to take their seats
support their canes
for a final farewell

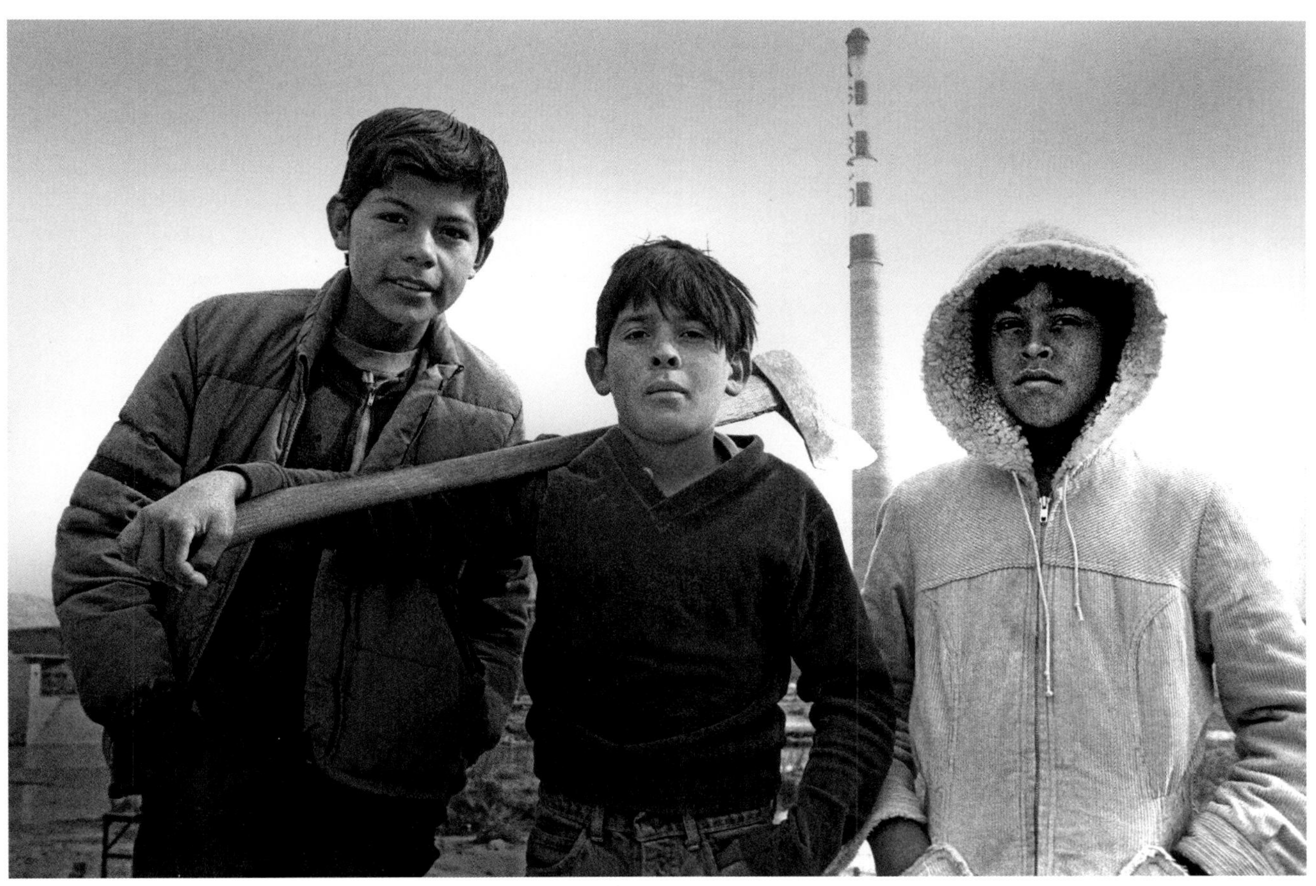

Three boys at the Rio. Juárez, Mexico, January 1, 2000.

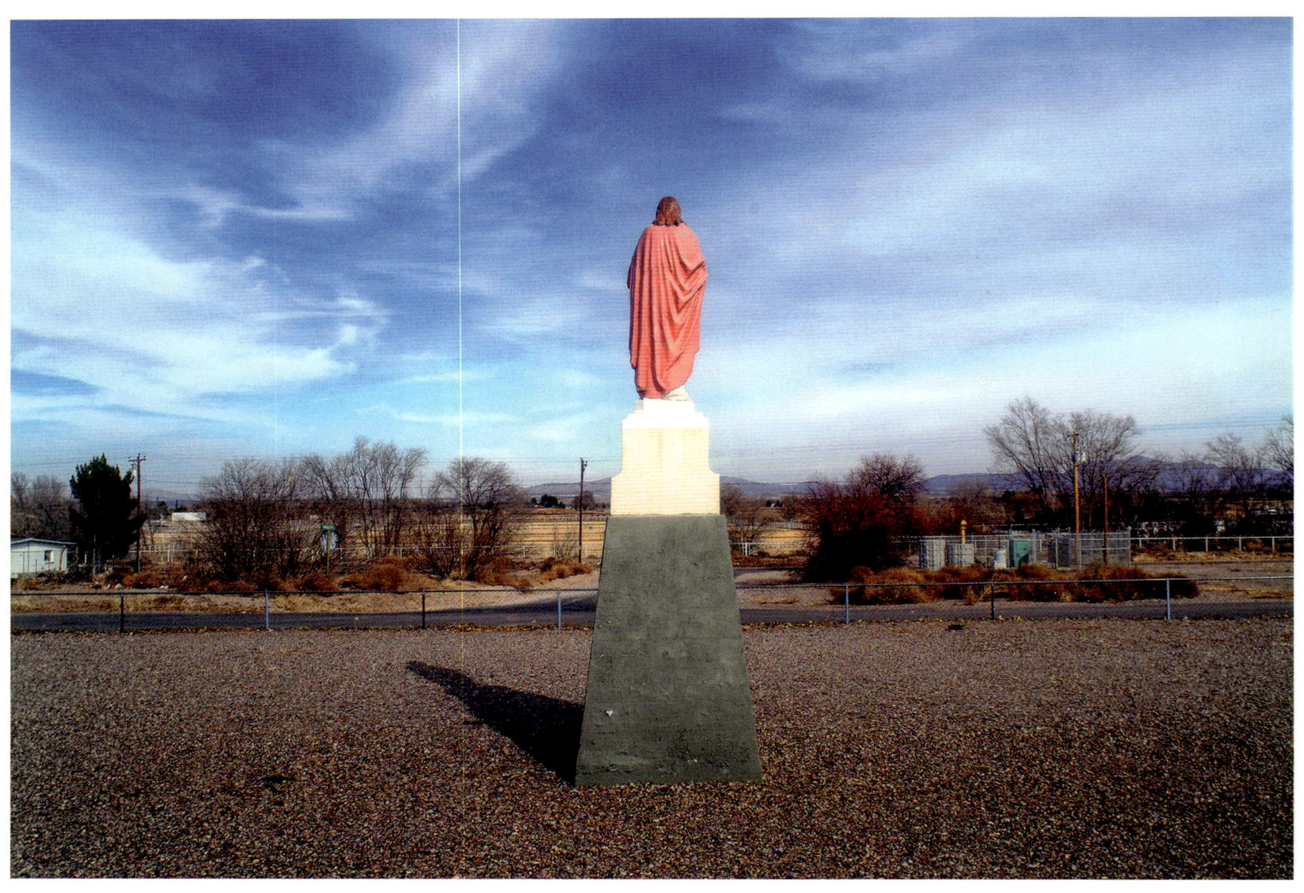

Jesus in the Mesilla Valley. New Mexico, 2002.

The Initiate

become the desert
and a dream
of fitting in
through control
and surrender
to sun, shade
water
and not much else.
one thinks
of a church
or medicine wheel
with lodge dreams
and steam
from water on stones
rising up
and then no more
the i can't take it
the waiting
for a blank canvas
or page
the possibility
of a newness
to believe in

New Rosary

for todd moore

only air and castanets
to click like beads
going round
until the crucifixion
as a resting
with no resting in sight
we postpone
rise up with the blood
pretend we know
the walk
our feet covered
with ashes and thorn
our hands upwards
to the sun
our eyes blinded
by the flashes
of yellowed light

and then a beginning
again with curses
the solutions and so unknown
the dream of resurrection
with lying and seeking
and starting over again
for the path
the path remains
will remain as ghost
as whisper
as mortgaged for the faithful
to take and leave
and remember what it gives:
questions and more deliverance
and grace
a collapsing too
for fate and eyes
and no easy exits
out a final door

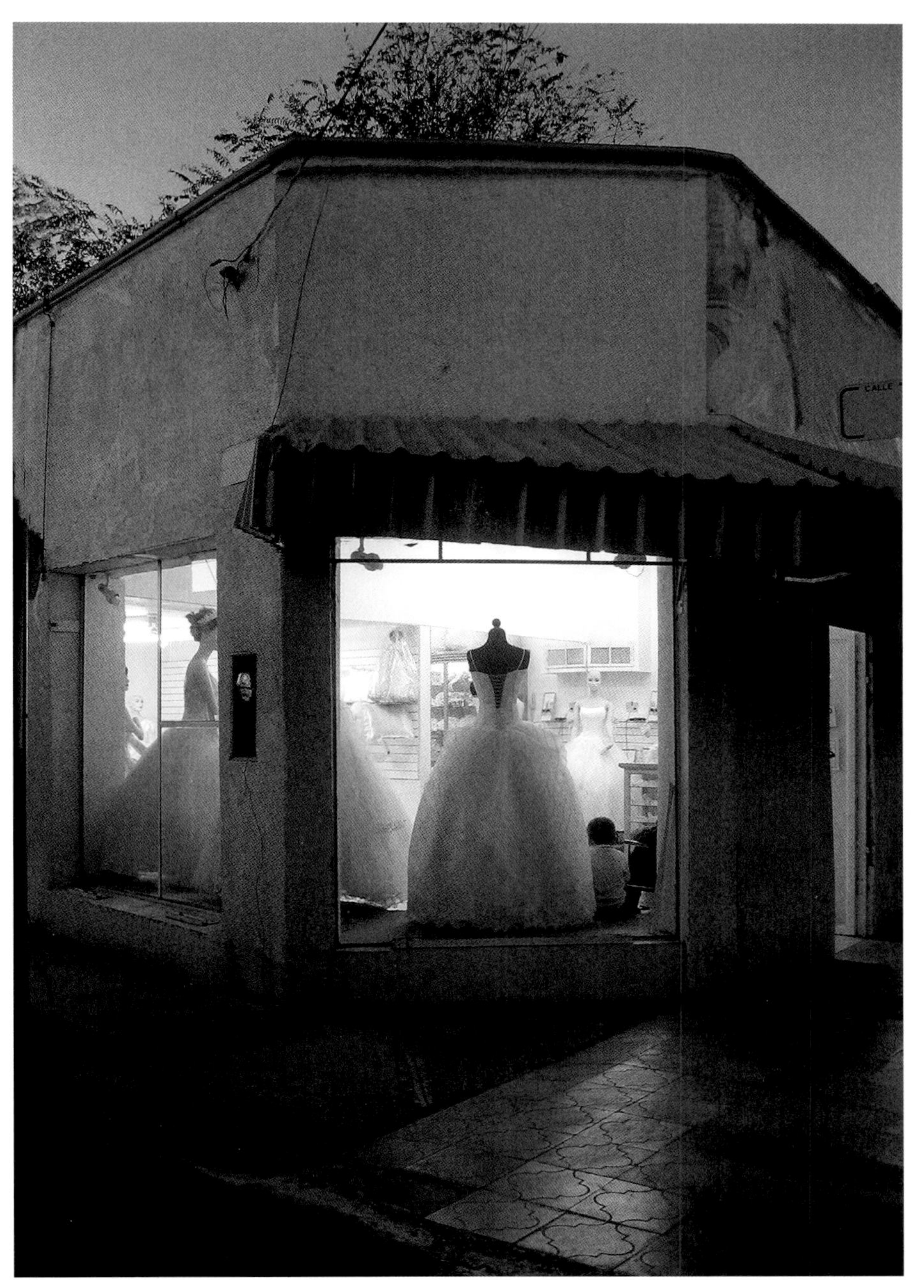

Calle Lerdo. Juárez, Mexico, 2005.

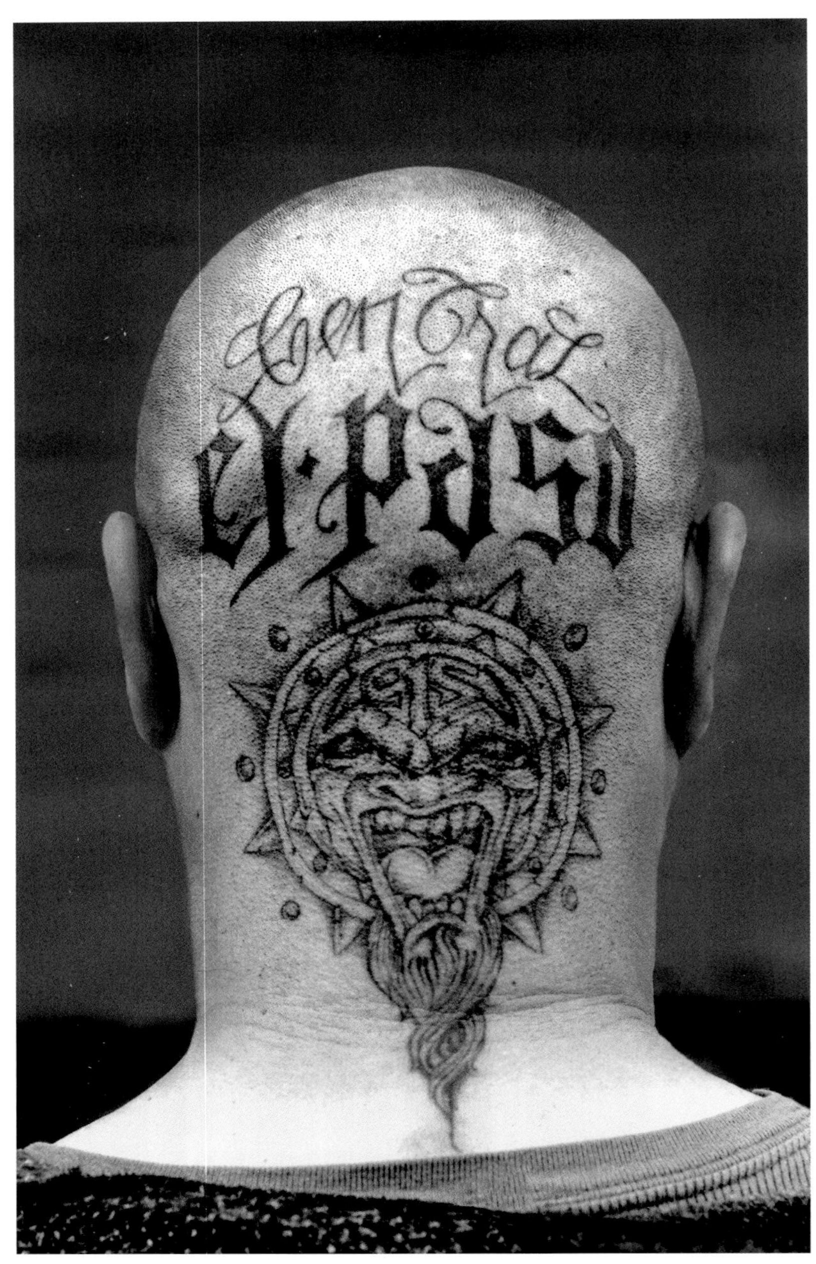

Central El Paso. El Paso, Texas, 2005.

Border Light

anapra hustler
hustles the mesa
to begin the other side
or sees the black fence
or blankness
for wandering eyes.
then unseen
as majesty
or flamed disappointment
he maneuvers
snips the wire
watches the light fade
and then
goes out

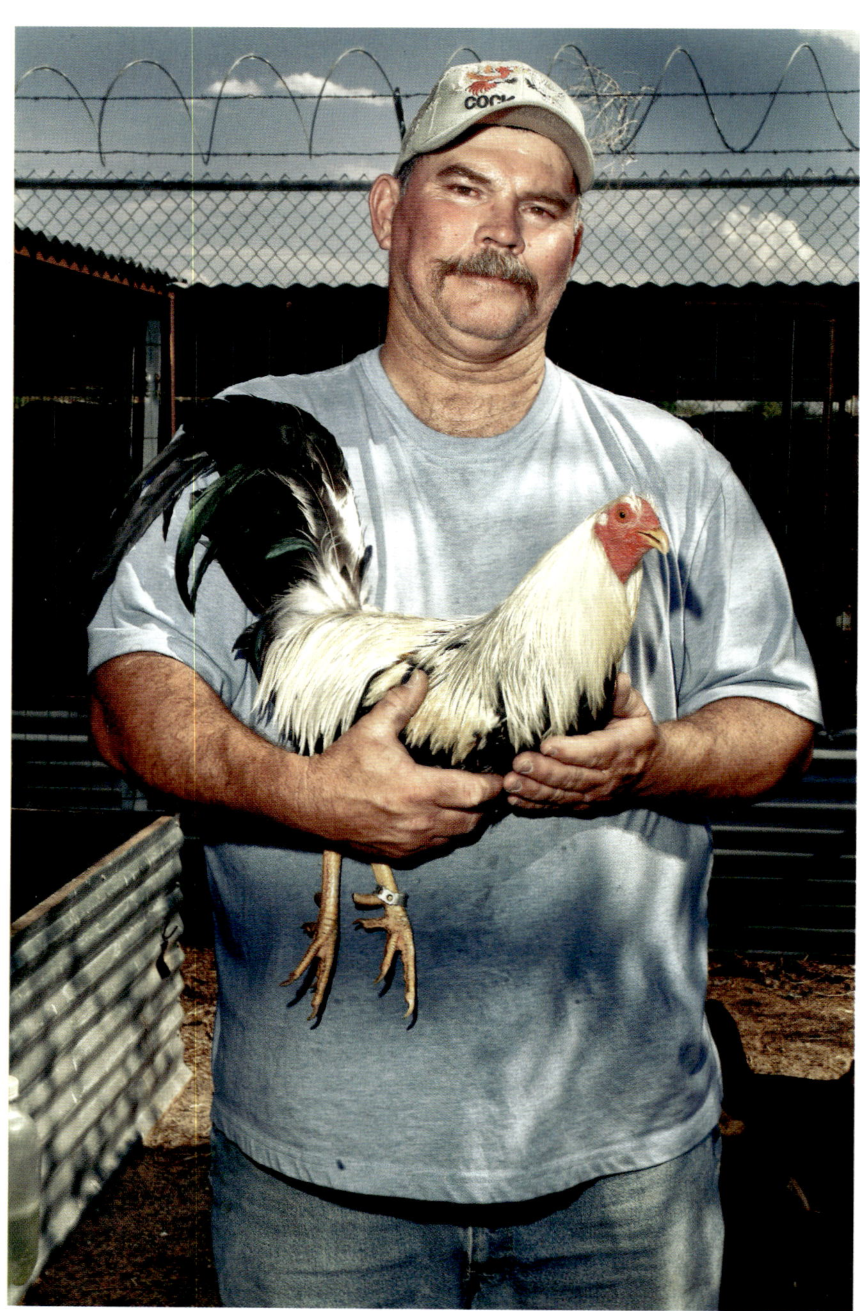

The last of the cockfighters. Chapparal, New Mexico, 2007.

Wolf and Sunflower

water
in turn
water
in turn
from a hose
only now
to help
the desert
and all that
remains dry.
at least
an existence
that's priceless
as they soak up
play to become
a dying song
that's captured
or realized in
a penitent's
melody

Dyer

spilled tokay
on concrete

the la caretta
lounge

or el dorado's
softened shout.

last chance
resurrects

old habits:
a grasping

for chilled
glass.

maybe mickey's
or the wagon

wheel north
toward chaparral

are never
remembered.

just the beauty
of confusion

the anonymous
spinning lights

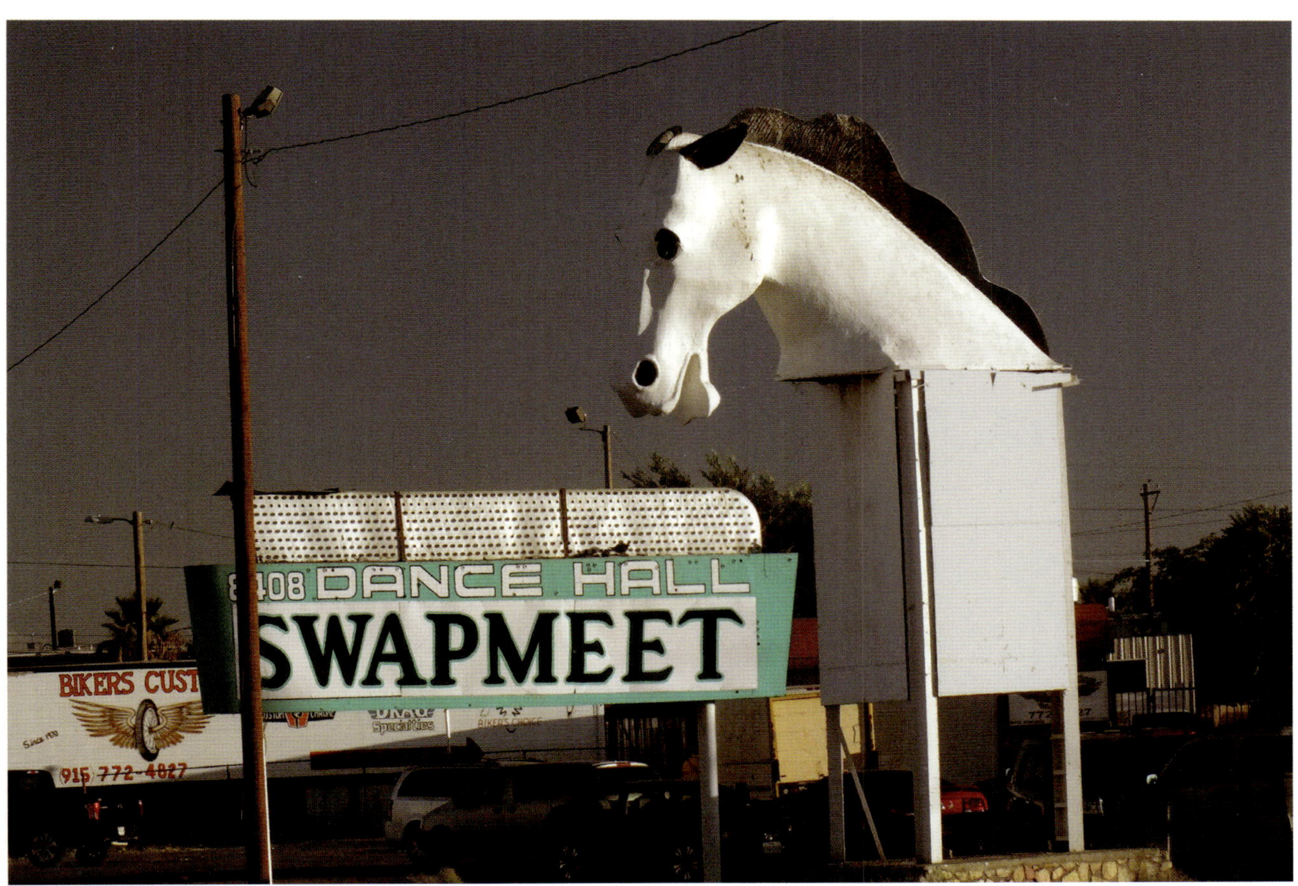

Luis's Bronco. El Paso, Texas, 2017.

Puro Oro Grande

pick up
the moon
on federal
land
or coyote's
plea
to savor
what
washes
our lives
even if "our"
is a cop-out

so then "me"
w/ a paper bag
me
hoping to pick
only sage
to stuff
my eyes
w/ puro oro grande
to let it
clean
w/ smoke
my only
reply

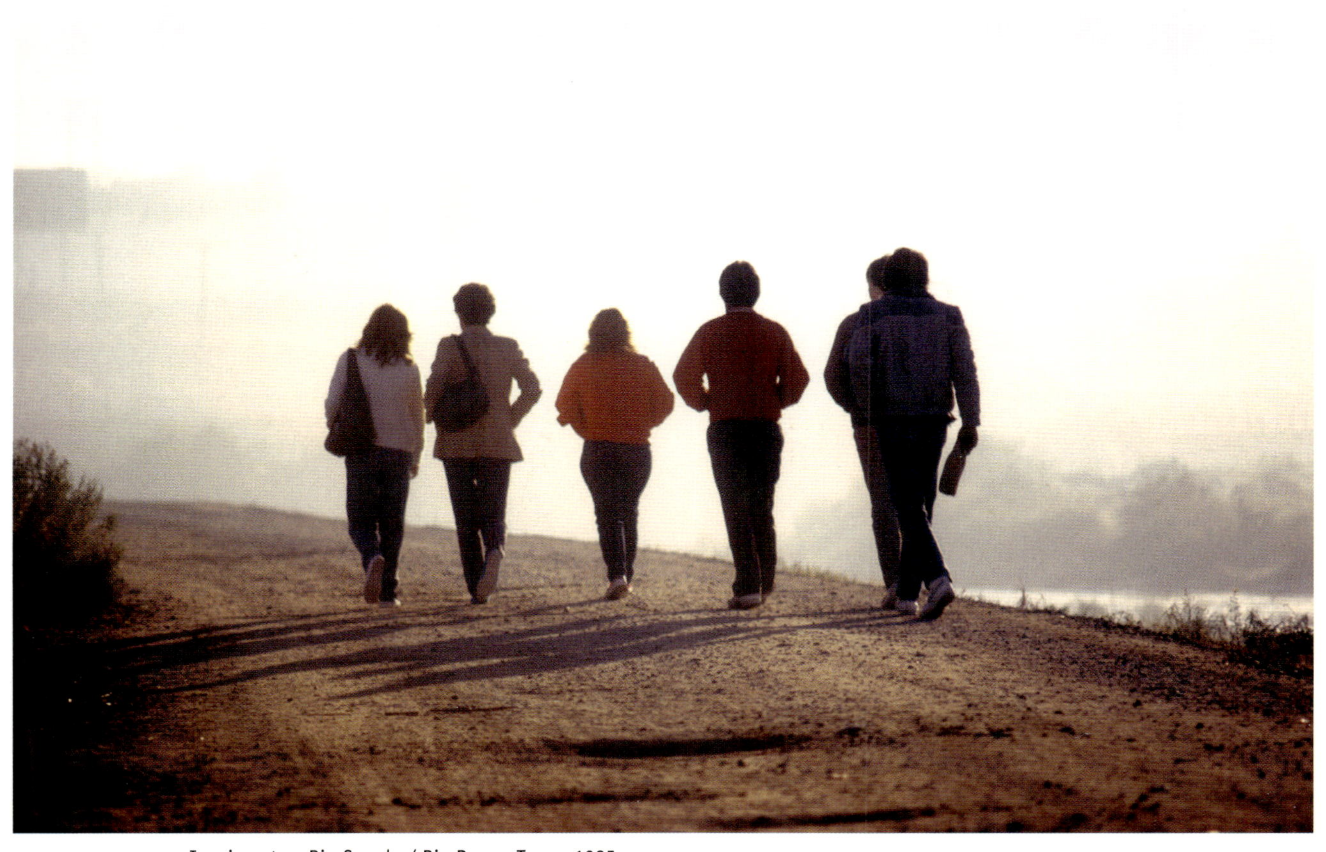

Immigrantes. Rio Grande / Rio Bravo, Texas, 1985.

Yellow Carnations / Day of the Dead

petal
trail
regresses
to
push:
flower
crucifix
of the
orange
gourd:
flash
strobe
for "other"
or
santos
as owls

they whisper

the owls
are here

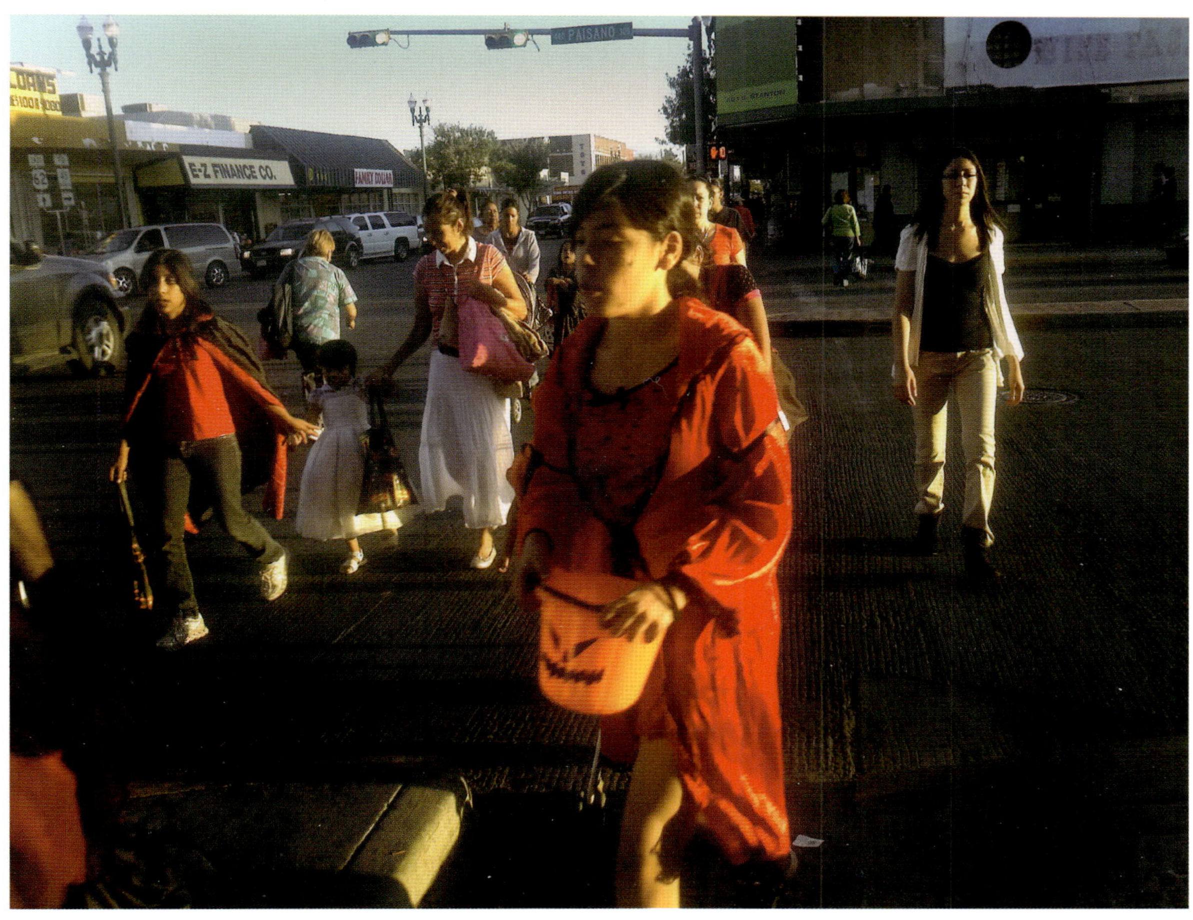

Barrio trick or treat. El Paso, Texas, 2012.

A Bath for Oro Grande

the borax cleanser
for worth to whisper
for will always give
what it can
of oro grande
that ghost town pitch.
enter while nothing's left
like lover
or water
or the empty pans of gold.
here
ajax speaks volumes
like busted locks
or the schoolhouse door
wide open.
take our graffiti
and crayons
our belts and christmas
bulbs
create the vat
fire hose the tub
for only the scrubbing
the scrubbing

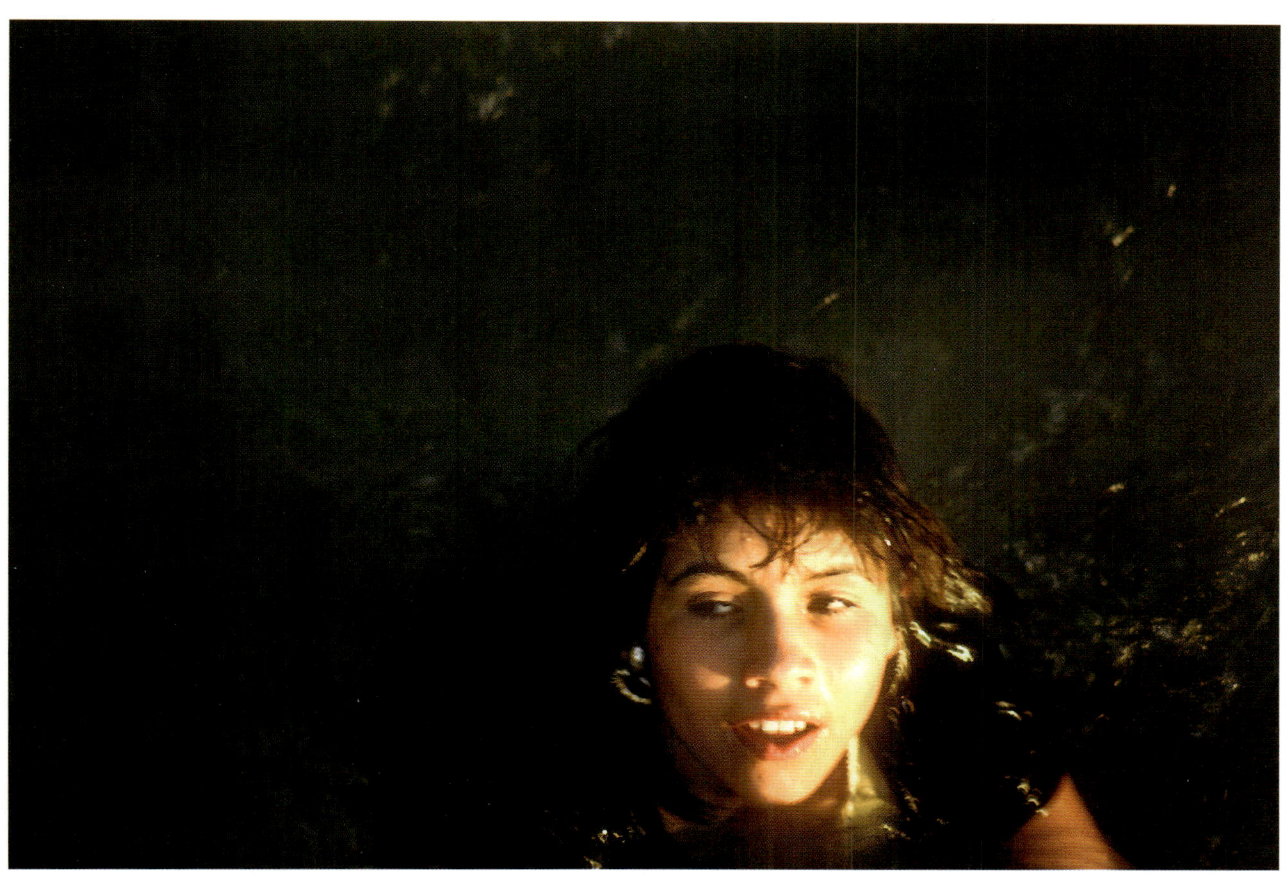

Girl with earring. Rio Grande / Rio Bravo, Texas, 1987.

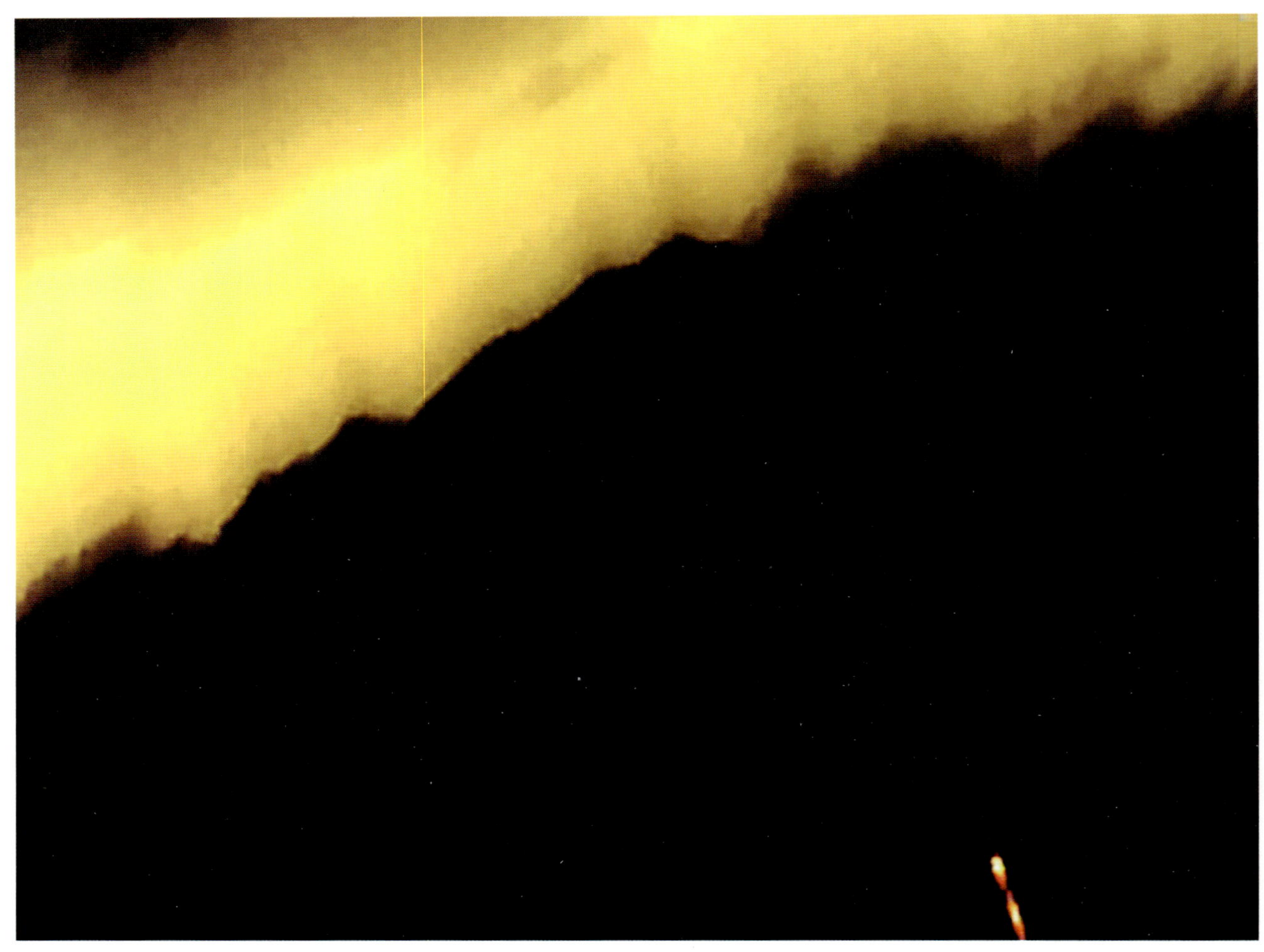

Mountain fire. El Paso, Texas, 2012.

El Paso Smelter at Night, 1919

after Freemont Ellis

how removed
by the flame
until all fires
burn inside a mind
and turn to slag
that forever glows
in no disappearance
the words
"american refinery"
will go all night
with only smoke, ash
its own thunder
in the morning light

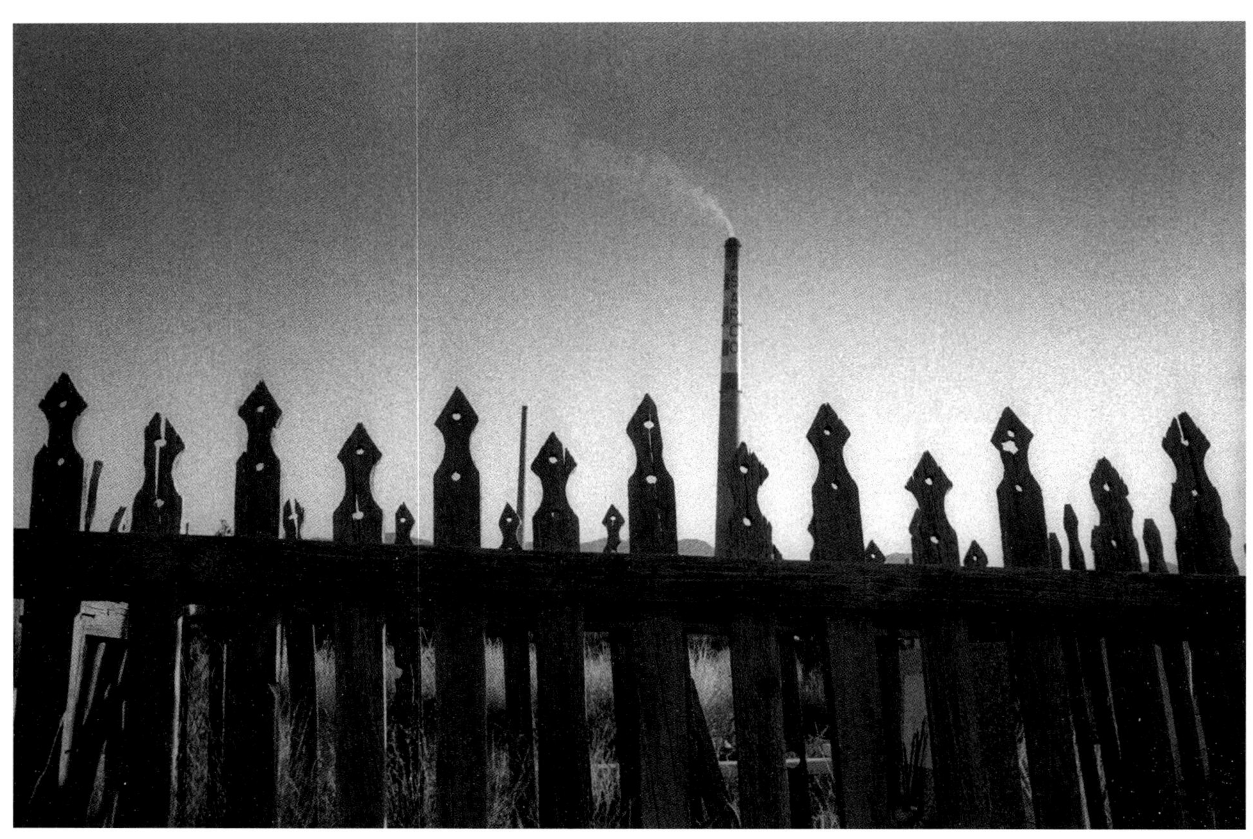

ASARCO and cemetery. El Paso, Texas, 1979.

Ghosts of Asarco

drumming
at the chain link
must remain
as slag's release
for smoke
going up
or none
as clouds
not down
the stacks
just whispers
of jobs
that pay
and pay well
and close
forever
behind
barbed wire
and padlocked gates

The Gutting of Wildhare's

royal crown review
shot back lot trash:

no strength to stand
or dale watson's lonestar

groove forced to move
beyond el paso

but where's that?
dragways to albuquerque's

promise of little action
or no race at all?

some say sleepy la beef
slept here or wayne

the train hancock scored
red pills to wash

the blues away. but
wreckers and cranes

dump trucks and busted
pool cues are the songs

off key, somehow
lost in the chihuahuan air

somehow blown through
and out the back end

but will they rise? they'll
never go away at all

as stamped to the desert wind
as a mesa shadow

as permanent as the lobo
now long gone

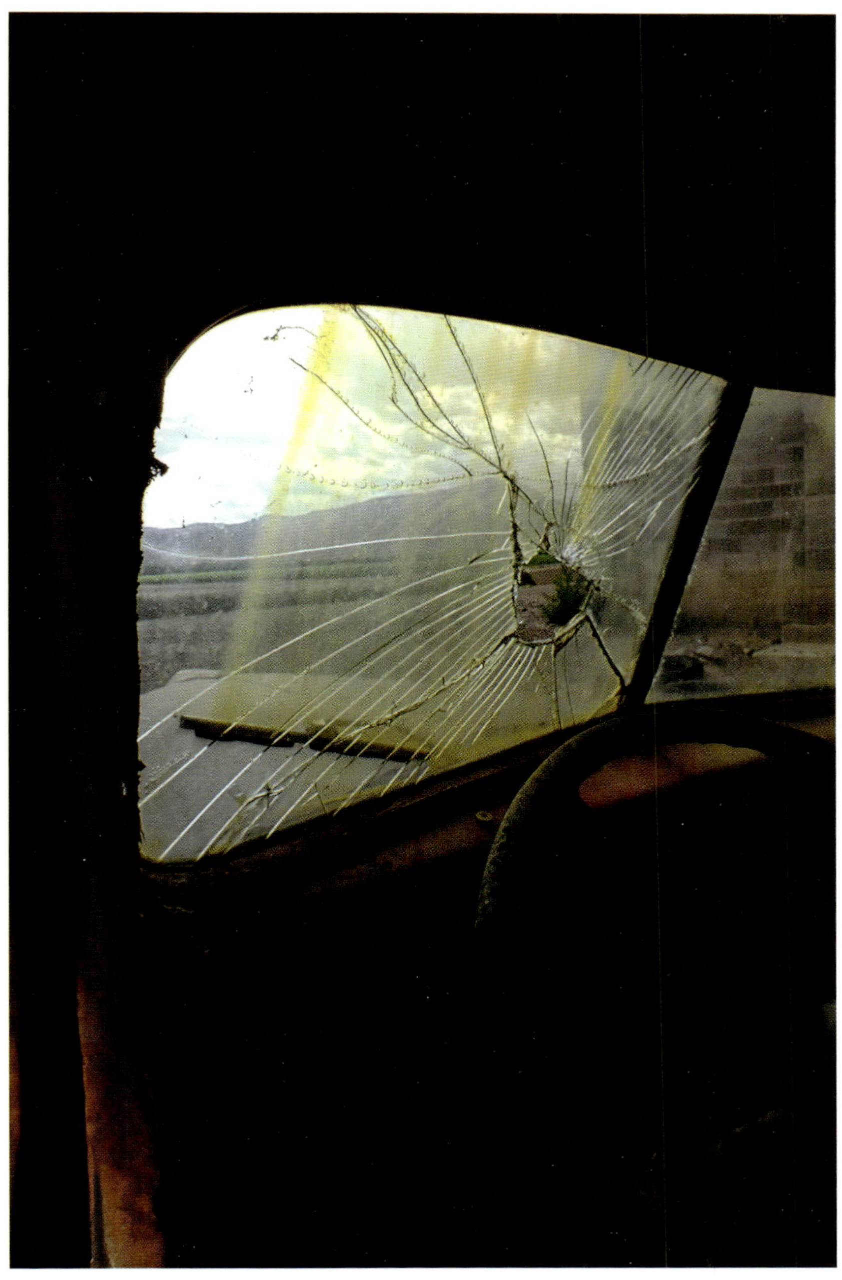

De Soto. Arrey Derry, New Mexico, 2010.

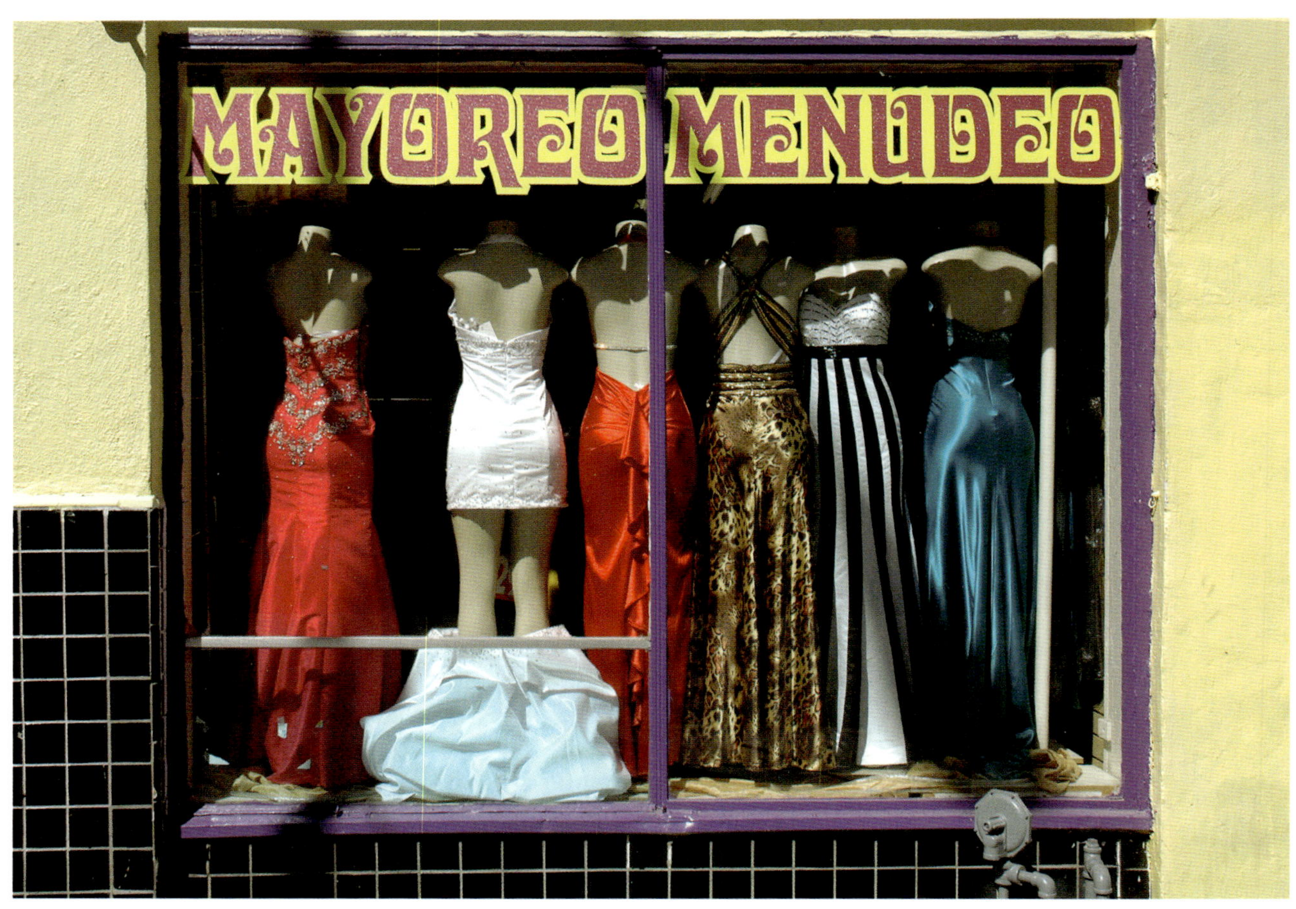

Wholesale/Retail. El Centro, El Paso, Texas, 2003.

Where the Boys Are

mountain shadows
at 108 degrees
become bones of those
unable to perform
at will
or under constraints
of the prescribed codes.
should they come out
now or ever
for a picking
for a teasing
for expectations?
oh they never will
or want.
so leave them
alone to remain
unable to view
unable to succeed
to pressures that never were
only a mind
they guess
as phantoms
on their way

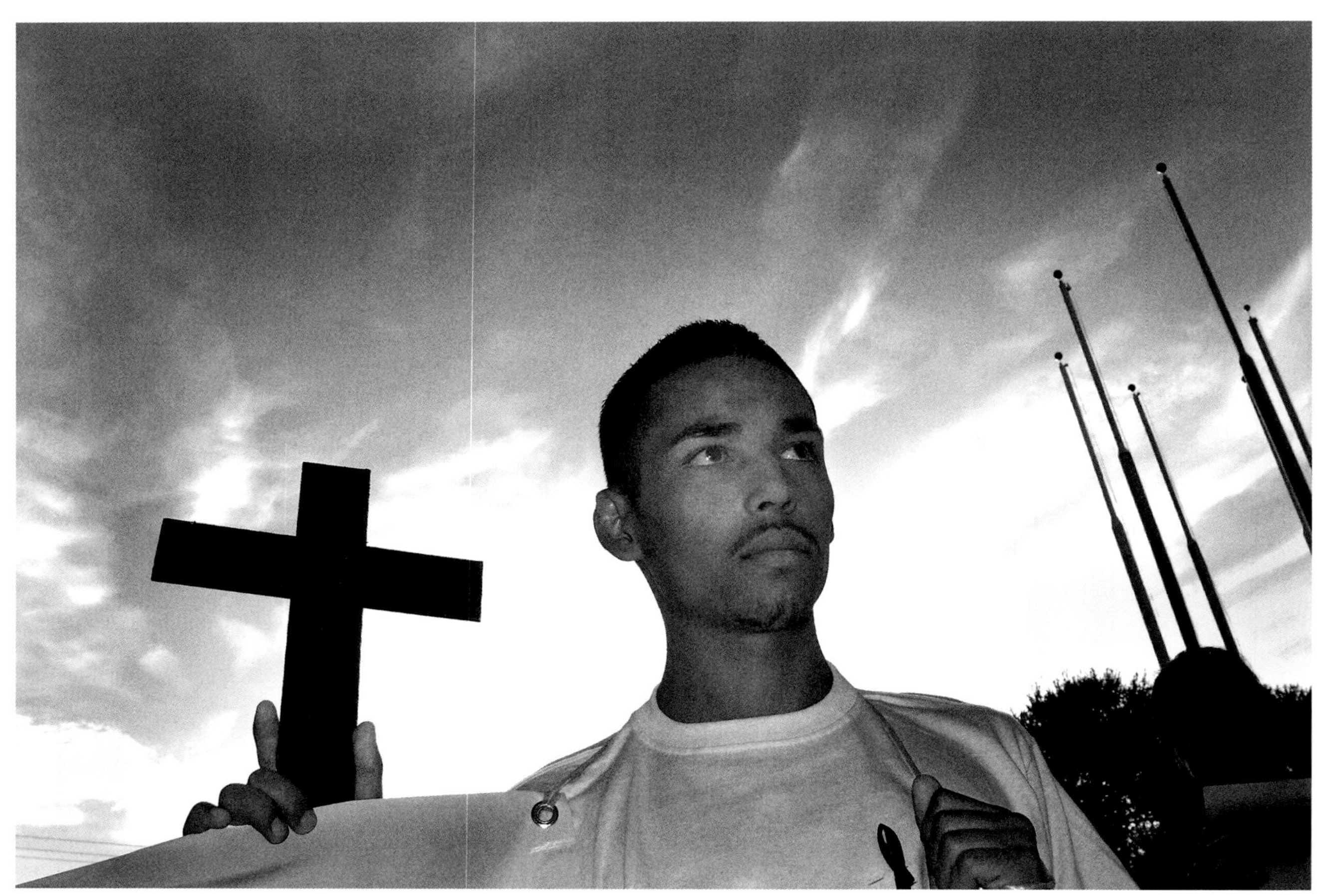

Black cross. Juárez, Mexico, 2009.

After the Sons of Villa

for Chris Smith and Erick "Chuco" Chavez

1
el paso's skull avenue or street is raynor
in cinco puntos
where the garage door rolls up or out
or the hideaway lounge holds treasures
not buried bones or sun, dust and sand
but remnants of a giving:
some modernism to know "place" like shards of sunset heights:
the sundowner apartments
asarco's smelter, madero and villa's grave
or a cottonwood encampment that hid them all

2
some new cumbia or juárez blood
is chihuahuan stamped to sing the roots of el paso high
austin high
bowie high
he claims with a camera for segundo barrio
turns to stilled canon images to flash
and release a torment of their own sound
for this is what we want: the purity of place
not new york, los angeles
but el paso in the non rhyme
the rhythm's fender amplification
or a jaded and wrecked microphone chord going in and out of today

3

now the charge is new gigs but where:
the either or lounge
take 2
wildhare's
or the east hollywood sewers where at 4 a.m. we sleep on the beaches
  of santa monica?

4

god please watch over these men and women
as they pack up and slip into the back rooms of red lights
let them take on stillness for black leather
white stetson hats that shade the 107 degree heat
their eyes protected from the blistering sun, sand and names
that will own the avenue
become its pitch and the essence that they were here forever
and never really there for the historians to see

5

now sons carry illuminations like suns for the decades and daughters
  who sing and dance too for purity or soul
it never hides when one acknowledges
the sound like lorca perhaps
or was it ricardo sanchez who paved the streets
w/ burciaga and mccarthy's blinding end

we forget about the big questions
they've already been answered and spin around like dust devils
like the first glimpse of a phoenix rising, rising
and a daybreak at dawn
and dusk for illuminations now
and continuations are all that we see

Old Border Highway Blues

madero's camp
enlivens asarco
or shuts its door
to slag
or what remains of ruin—
an escape
towards the new mexico line
where the rio grande
serves as runoff
demarcation for
cottonwood trackers
those shade keepers known
genuflect and disappear
across the anapra line

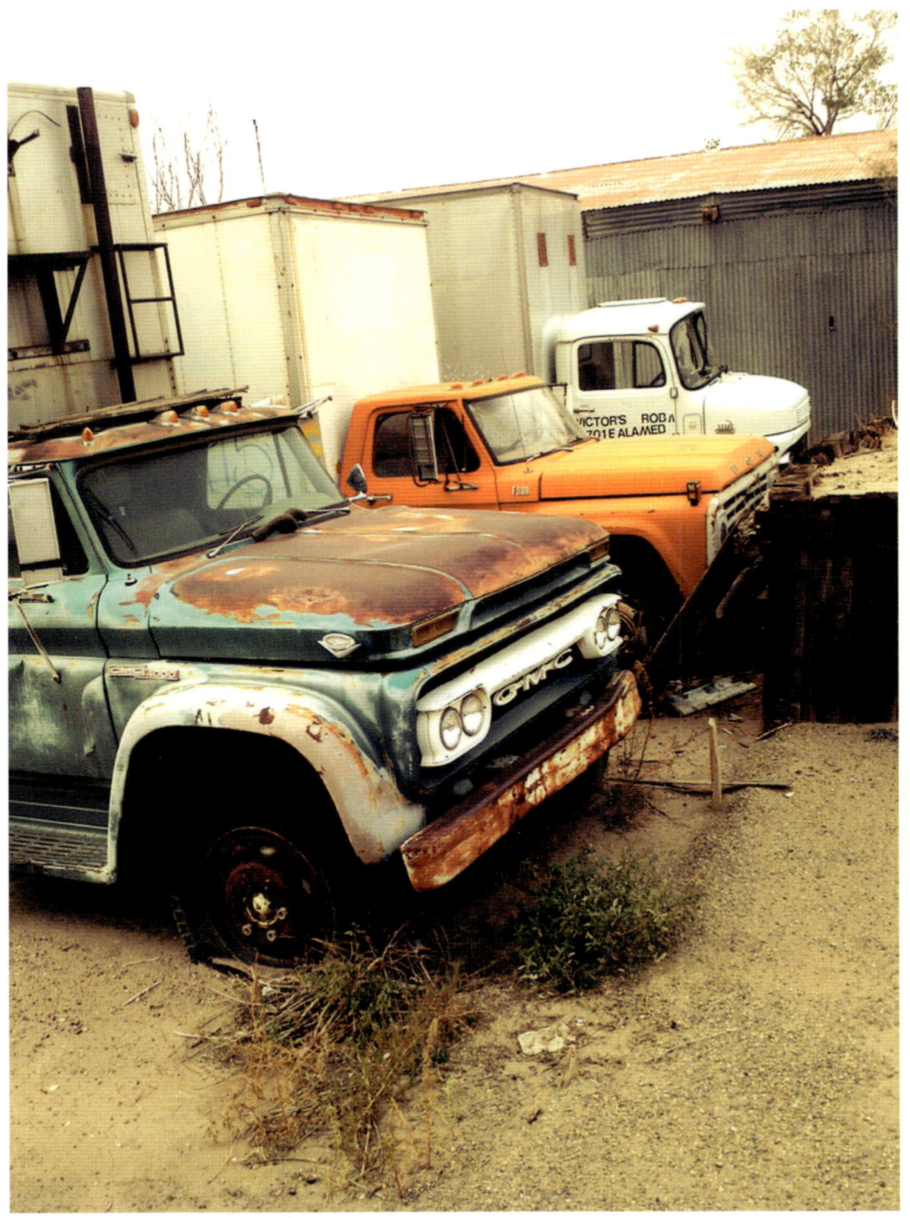

Tired trucks. Chamizal, El Paso, Texas, 2012.

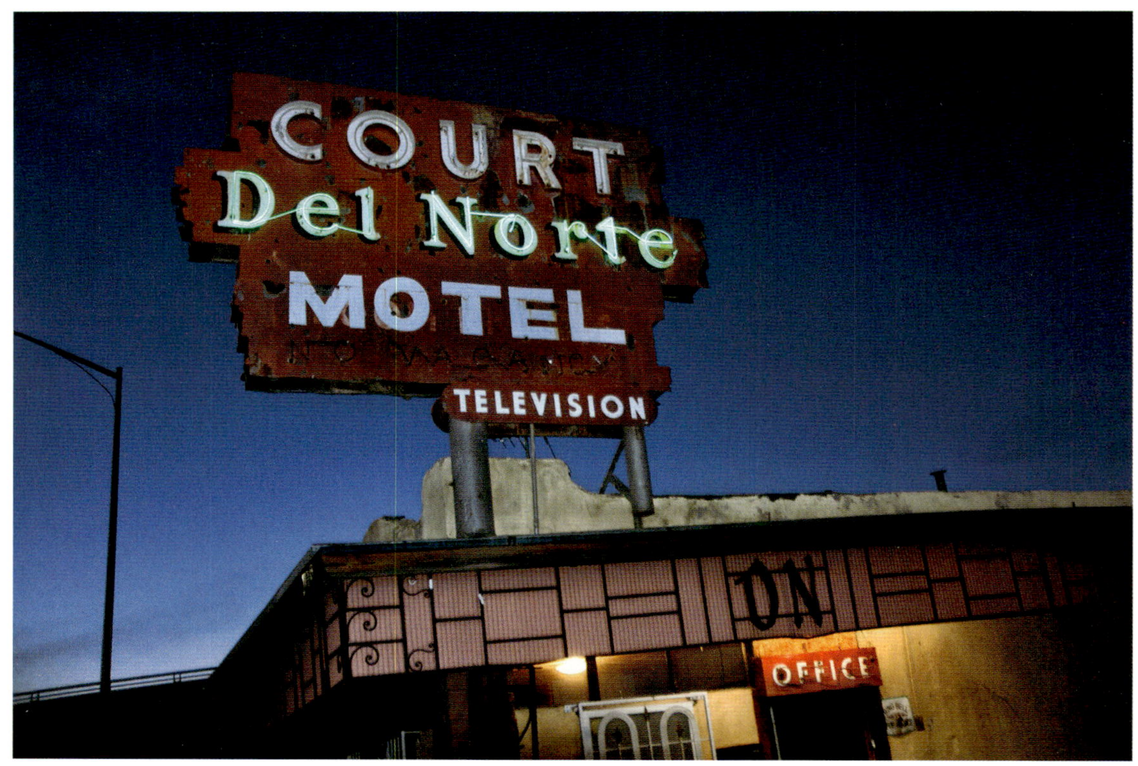

Del Norte Court. El Paso, Texas, 2016.

Somewhere in Texas

shadows or is it light
on the steps disappearing
under overhead fans
as the people remain
on worn-out sofas
and become some border
like a racetrack or casino
down the road with free
drinks on sunday
for the mariachi musicians
and those who listen
watch the mountains
and they too as shadows
now and then disappear
become no more
with a whisper
or last call
at midnight

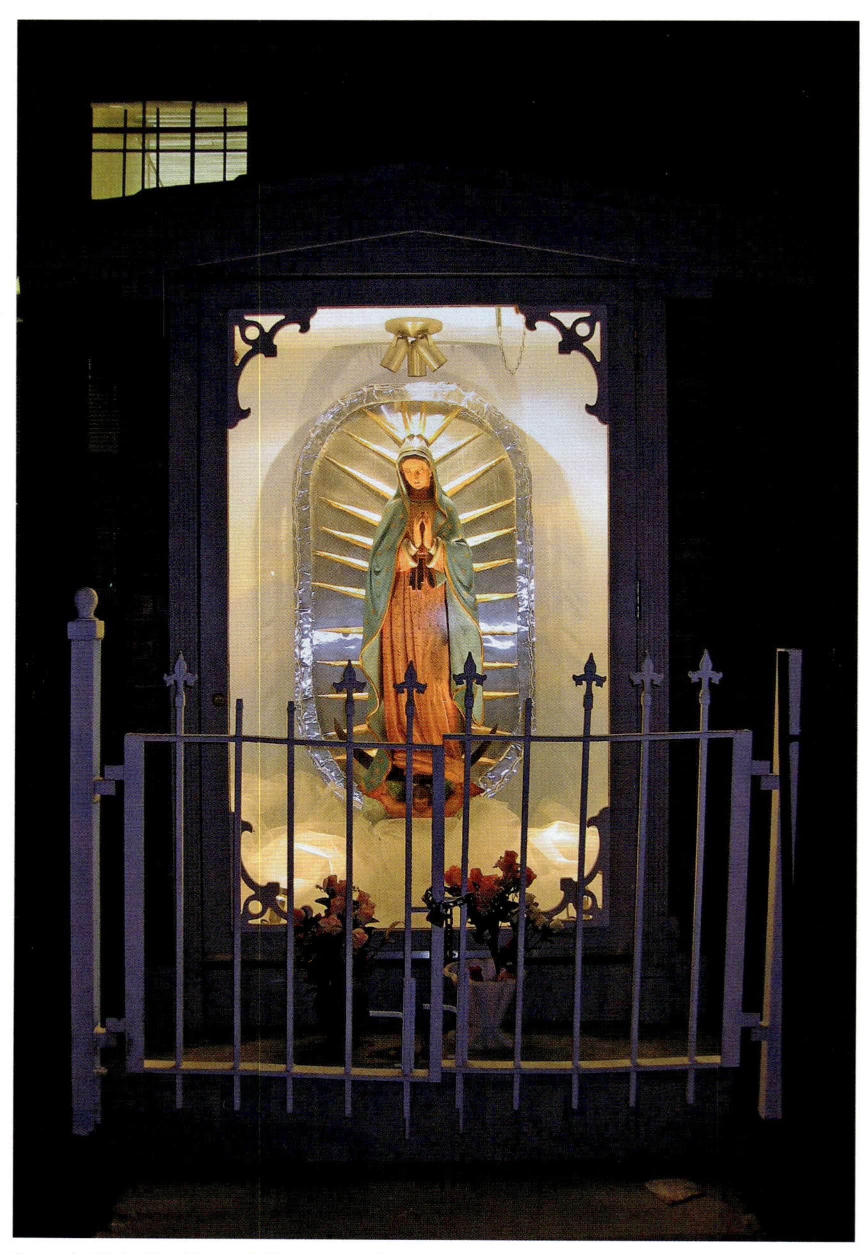

Segundo Night Guadalupe, El Paso, Texas, 2006.

CONTRIBUTORS

Bruce Berman has been a professional photographer for over five decades and has always worked in the documentary style, what some call the "Concerned Photographer" style of photography. Additionally, he has over twenty years of experience teaching in higher education.

His initial documentary projects were in Chicago, where he photographed Appalachian migrants in Uptown, Black Panthers during the tumultuous late 1960s, and the gritty street life of Chicago in its Rust Belt years. During these tumultuous years he was Midwest photographer for the *Christian Science Monitor* and freelanced for the AP, UPI, *Chicago Tribune*, the *New York Times*, *Time*, *Newsweek*, *Der Spiegel*, the *Bulletin of the Atomic Scientists*, and others.

His main work for the past thirty years has concentrated on the US-Mexico border, particularly the narrow stretch of land that encompasses El Paso, Texas, and Juárez, Mexico. Starting in 2007, his work has turned more and more to traditional documentary photojournalism, the form that he began with. As he said in a recent interview, "Photojournalism is the only form I can think of that really can tell what La Frontera is today." Bruce Berman's work has appeared in the *New York Times*, *Time*, and other national and international publications and on his own online magazine, the Border Blog (www.border-blog.com).

Since 2006 he has been a professor at New Mexico State University, where he teaches Introduction to Photography, Documentary Photography, and Photojournalism. His undergraduate and graduate degrees were earned at the University of Oklahoma H. H. Herbert School of Journalism, and he studied with Ernst Hass of Magnum, Sam Abell of *National Geographic*, and Roy Morsch of the *New York Daily News*.

Berman's work at NMSU has concentrated on making the learning experience as "real world" as possible. "Being a photojournalist is all about improvisation and commitment," he says. "Once you have the basics you have to teach yourself your own tricks, find your own voice, improve your listening and your seeing skills, and realize the extent of the commitment that is required to get to a meaningful outcome." He often tells his students, "I want you to use photography as an instrument of education, not self-expression, so that you will have a chance to matter."

He tries to follow that advice.

Ray Gonzalez is the author of numerous books of poetry, including six from BOA Editions—*The Heat of Arrivals* (PEN/Oakland Josephine Miles Book Award), *Cabato Sentora* (Minnesota Book Award Finalist), *The Hawk Temple at Tierra Grande* (Minnesota Book Award for Poetry), *Consideration of the Guitar: New and Selected Poems*, *Cool Auditor: Prose Poems*, and *Beautiful Wall* (Minnesota Book Award for Poetry). The University of Arizona Press published eight of his books, including *Turtle Pictures* (Minnesota Book Award for Poetry), a mixed-genre text. His poems have appeared in the 1999, 2000, 2003, and 2014 editions of *The Best American Poetry* and *The Pushcart Prize: Best of the Small Presses 2000*.

He is the author of three collections of essays, *The Underground Heart: A Return to a Hidden Landscape*, which received the Carr P. Collins / Texas Institute of Letters Award for Best Book of Non-fiction; *Memory Fever*; and *Renaming the Earth: Personal Essays*. He has written two collections of short stories, *The Ghost of John Wayne* (Western Heritage Award for Best Short Story and Latino Heritage Award in Literature) and *Circling the Tortilla Dragon*.

He is the editor of twelve anthologies, most recently *Sudden Fiction Latino: Short-Short Stories from the United States and Latin America*. He received a 2017 Witter Bynner Fellowship from the Library of Congress and chosen by the US poet laureate. In 1998 he founded *LUNA*, a poetry journal, which received a Fund for Poetry grant for Excellence in Publishing. He was awarded a 2015 Con Tinta Lifetime Achievement Award in Latino Literature and a 2002 Lifetime Achievement Award from the Southwest Border Regional Library Association. He is a professor in the MFA Creative Writing Program at the University of Minnesota in Minneapolis.

Born and raised in South Central Los Angeles, **Lawrence Welsh** lives in El Paso, Texas. A first-generation Irish American and award-winning journalist, Welsh has published ten books of poetry, including *Begging for Vultures: New and Selected Poems, 1994–2009* (University of New Mexico Press). Now in a second printing, this collection won the New Mexico–Arizona Book Award. It was also named a Notable Book by Southwest Books of the Year and was a finalist for both the PEN Southwest Book Award and the Writers' League of Texas Book Award.

A winner of the Bardsong Press Celtic Voice Writing Award in Poetry and the 2017 *Pen World* magazine Montegrappa essay competition, Welsh is an English professor at El Paso Community College. He has also lectured, read, and taught at a wide range of universities and institutions, including UCLA, New Mexico State University, the University of Texas at El Paso, the University of Missouri–St. Louis, and Murray State University. His journalism awards include the Society of Professional Journalists Bill Farr Reporting Award, the Copley Los Angeles Newspapers Award, the Jessie Steensma Endowment Scholarship, and the Women in Communications Endowment Award.

In 2011 *Irish America* magazine in New York City named him one of the "Top 100 Irish Americans" of the year. In 1987 he received the Society of Professional Journalists / Sigma Delta Chi Outstanding Graduating Journalist Award from California State University, Long Beach. In 1979 he cofounded the Alcoholics, the L.A. punk rock band. As part of its Punk Archive Series, Sahlugg Records of Los Angeles in 2017 released *East of Sepulveda: 1979–1982*, a retrospective of the band's studio and live cuts.

Welsh's poetry, fiction, reviews, essays, and journalistic writings have appeared in more than two hundred national, international, and regional magazines, journals, newspapers, and anthologies, including *Puerto del Sol*, *Hawaii Review*, the *Louisiana Review*, the *Rio Grande Review*, the *Texas Observer*, the *Santa Fe New Mexican*, the *Irish Echo*, *Irish America*, the *Honest Ulsterman*, the *New Madrid Review*, the *Wormwood Review*, *Onthebus*, *Pearl*, *Poetry Now*, *Big Bridge*, the *Café Review*, *Nexus*, *Chiron Review*, *Poetry Motel*, *Main Street Rag*, the *Powhatan Review*, *Pitchfork*, and the Los Angeles *Daily Breeze*, the 2015 Pulitzer Prize–winning newspaper where he spent five years as a reporter and staff writer in the 1980s.

A native Texan, **Lisa McNiel** was born and raised in El Paso. A graduate of Trinity University in San Antonio with a BA in English, she also holds a master's degree in Theater from the University of Texas at El Paso. A published poet, McNiel is an associate professor of Speech at El Paso Community College and also served as the Speech and Theater Coordinator. In 2012 EPCC nominated her for the Minnie Stevens Piper Professor award, and she received the National Institute for Staff and Organizational Development Excellence in Teaching award. During the past decade, McNiel has given numerous leadership and esteem-building workshops for the community, including the Rio Grande Cancer

Foundation and the City of El Paso Museum and Cultural Affairs Department. She also has been a member of both the National Communication Association and the Theta Iota Chapter of Delta Kappa Gamma, a service and honor society for women in education. In the realm of theater, McNiel has directed more than twenty plays and acted in a wide range of roles in local productions, including Dorine in *Tartuffe* and Fastrada in *Pippin*.

David Dorado Romo is an essayist, historian, and translator. He is the author of *Ringside Seat to a Revolution: An Underground Cultural History of El Paso and Juárez, 1893–1923*. His book received several awards in 2006, including the Texas Writer's League Violet Crown, the Western Literature Association Book of the Year, the Western Writer's of America Spur Award, the Border Regional Library Association Southwest Book Award, and the Latino Literacy Now International Book Award. His published translations include *Questions and Swords* by Subcomandante Marcos and *Soldaderas* by Elena Poniatowska. Romo, a former Fulbright scholar, has studied at the Hebrew University of Jerusalem and Stanford University, and he obtained his doctorate in borderland history from the University of Texas at El Paso. He is currently a resident scholar at the School for Advanced Research in Santa Fe, New Mexico. He is working on his next book, *Mexican Nazis and Global Pachucos: Propaganda, Intelligence, and the Production of Border Invasion Anxiety*. His essays and reviews have appeared in both *Texas Monthly* and *The Texas Tribune*.